MMM2

Modern Music Masters – Blur

Tom Boniface-Webb

Modern Music Masters

ISBN: 978-1-8381887-1-9
modernmusicmastersuk@gmail.com

DEDICATION

This book is dedicated to Jenny, for all the times we enjoyed listening to, watching and talking about, Blur.
Happy birthday

CONTENTS

ACKNOWLEDGMENTS

Thank you to all the following, without whom this book would not have been possible:

Cover Design: Barry Parkinson at www.beepea.co.uk
Advice, support and good vibes: Jenny Natasha
eBook publishing: Lisa Liu
The Society of Authors
www.discogs.com
Special thanks to the UK Official Charts Company, the most invaluable resource for this book series

Books in the Modern Music Masters Series:

Oasis
Blur
Pulp
Manic Street Preachers
The Verve
Suede

MMM2 – Blur Spotify Playlist

Available at: MMM2 – Blur

FOREWORD:

So, what do we think of when we think of Blur?

As is the case with so many British stories, the narrative of Blur's is one intrinsically tied to the British class system. To some, you say the name Blur and an image is conjured of cheeky cockney chappies sporting Adidas Gazelles, flanked by Phil Daniels singing Parklife. To others they are the Middle England Champagne socialists, supporting Tony Blair, and propping up the bar at Soho House with Keith Allen, trading on fabricated working-class roots, mincing about in music videos made by Damian Hirst, and throwing copies of Balzac at the Gallagher brothers.

Both of these willfully constructed images are true, and both are fake. A band like Blur were many things to many people because they always worked hard to position themselves at the cutting edge of what it meant to be an indie-rock band in the nineties and beyond. From baggy also-rans, through serious British pin-ups, by the late nineties they finally shape-shifted into the more serious, grown-up group that we know them as today. A group just as interested in experimentation, in analogue keyboards that go 'bleep' just as much as guitars that go 'grr'.

Damon Albarn is the modern renaissance man of modern British music. His many musical projects, most notably the world's first fully animated group Gorillaz, could easily fill a whole volume of an MMM itself (and maybe will one day), but it was when playing alongside Graham Coxon, Alex James and Dave Rowntree, that Damon was always most at home. You can't help the music that you grow up with, no more than you can help the place you are born into, but it will always remain part of you, and for many of us, this means Blur are our band, and always will be.

Modern Music Masters – Blur is the second in the MMM series. It is a stand-alone book for all the die-hard Blur fans out there, or those new to the band looking for an overview, or it can be enjoyed as part of the growing series. At just over 50,000 words, this book doesn't pretend to be an exhaustive history of the band. Rather, the series is purposefully designed to act as something of an introduction.

As always, there are a range of fantastic books on Blur that can be enjoyed for a more full, in-depth, understanding of the band and their music. Those that I read whilst researching this book include: Damon Albarn: Blur, Gorillaz and Other Fables by Martin Roach and David Nolan (Music Press, 2015); The Life of Blur by Martin Power (Omnibus, 2013); the Britpop bible (alongside I Was Britpopped of course…) The Last Party: Britpop, Blair and the Demise of English Rock by John Harris (Harper Perennial, 2003); and of course, from the man who lived it and survived, Bit of a Blur by Alex James (Little and Brown, 2007). Much respect also goes to the directors of No Distance Left to Run, the ultimate Blur documentary, Will Lovelace and Dylan Southern (Pulse Films, 2010).

As before, there is a particular focus on the UK charts to help tell Blur's story. With the charts acting as an indicator for popularity, we can see how the band rode the wave of success and relevance through their chart placings, which has so far culminated in two number 1 singles (and two number 2s, that just missed out on the top spot), and five number 1 albums. Although a solid indicator of judging a band's popularity within the mainstream, the charts are not the be all and end all in analysing their success, and as such the idea was to try and position each of the band's key moments of importance as stepping stones to help tell their amazing story.

Once again, I hope you enjoy the journey with me.

Tom Boniface-Webb
November 2020

A FEW WORDS FROM THE AUTHOR

My first memory of Blur is when I asked a prospective girlfriend, my first prospective girlfriend, the question that you asked a prospective girlfriend in 1995: 'who do you prefer out of Blur and Oasis?' This would have been mid-December, about four months after the fateful chart clash between the two bands had divided the nation in August 1995. She told me she preferred Oasis, so I duly bought (What's the Story) Morning Glory?, and after one of the guys I hated most at school was given The Great Escape around the same time, it seemed obvious whose side I was on.

But my relationship with the band must have gone further back than that. I remember playing Girls & Boys on the common room stereo back in March 1994, and staying up late to watch footage of them playing at what must have been their huge Mile End show in June 1995. Just like Oasis, by the time Parklife was out in the world doing its thing, they slipped so seamlessly into the cultural fabric of the country that it was impossible not to know who they were.

At some point in 1995 I borrowed Parklife from the Caversham Library, taping it and playing it back until it was worn through. Away from the general promotion of the album – apart from Girls & Boys and Parklife, I had no idea what the singles had been – it felt like I had found the album and it was mine alone. I was drawn to the domesticity of Bank Holiday, which felt like a song about the BBQs that my family insisted on having every time there was a Monday off from work, and Badhead, perhaps because of – although, not known at the time – its story about depression, that would later on in adulthood also get me.

I liked the singles from The Great Escape, particularly The Universal, and listening to Stereotypes, I felt the exciting, embarrassed flush of watching a Carry On movie, hoping my parents didn't pick up on its message of wife-swapping when it played on the car radio. But as a whole, I thought The Great Escape was pretty rubbish. Partly because of the kid at school having it, partly because the band were done up as suave businessmen on the back cover, which totally did away with why I thought they were so cool, but mostly because the songs were not as good as those on Parklife.

By the time that Beetlebum came out, I was old enough (about to turn 16) and now knew enough about music to know it was a great song. They had ditched the pomposity of Country House and distilled the band to its core essence, which was playing their instruments and looking cool. Watching their performance on TFI Friday the week before the single came out, I just thought Damon was the coolest guy in the world, sat there strumming his acoustic, flanked by his expressionless bandmates, and I rushed out to buy the single, stupidly giving it to my first proper girlfriend (not the same one from earlier) as a present for Valentine's Day.

Blur Blur confused me. In parts it was so incredibly good, and in other parts it felt disorientating and hard to listen to. I particularly struggled with Theme from Retro and Death of a Party, but loved the singles and You're So Great, the latter teaching me that it was ok to sing vaguely off key sometimes, as long as the passion is there. I stuck with it though, and what had originally put me off, eventually became the standout moments on the album. They were trying something new, experimenting, which was much more than could be said for the other Britpop bands I was listening to at the time.

When 13 came out in 1999, it was clear that Blur were the best band in the world. More accessible than Radiohead, more adventurous than Oasis or the Manic Street Preachers, and with Damon as their lead singer and spokesperson, clearly the best-looking band out there.

I saw them for the first time at the famous Reading Festival performance in 1999 when Damon announced they would be taking some time off, whilst telling us stories of being given ecstasy on their first Top of the Pops performance, and making us say the word 'hoses' over and over, for some reason. I think it was probably the best gig I had ever been to, and I rushed to buy tickets to the singles concert in October 1999, trekking up the M40 to Birmingham, and earning myself a speeding ticket for my troubles.

Unlike Oasis, my love affair with Blur only deepened as time went on. It was incredibly sad that Graham was kicked out when he was, but it meant that his solo material got better and better, and the quiet, thoughtfulness of Think Tank acted as a suitable counter-point to the hectic garage-rock of The Libertines that was so popular then. I even caught them, Graham-less, at 2003's Reading Festival, but it wasn't the same, they tried, and songs still sounded good, but something had been broken, and would need a lot of work to be fixed.

And then suddenly it was fixed. 2009 came about and we all jumped on the Piccadilly Line to Hyde Park Corner on 2nd July for the homecoming, reunion concert of our lives. And then it seemed like we blinked and it was 2012 and all happening again. Blur, our band, were part of the Cultural Olympiad, and that meant we were connected to the proceedings in a way that we might have missed out on otherwise. It was a clever move by the Tony Hall and Danny Boyle, and one that paid off.

I must admit to having not listened to The Magic Whip too much when it first came out. It's a good album, but as life goes on, other factures become more important. There is only so much space for new music, and the eighth album by a band I loved when I was 18 didn't seem as important as listening to an up and coming artist; but listening to it back for this book, I realise that it is both a great and necessary addition to the Blur canon, but also, that it is just good music, that I should have made the effort to listen to more over the last five years. I won't make that mistake again.

Gorillaz are a great band, just as Graham's solo albums are also great. But nothing quite compares to the feeling that you get when listening to a band that meant something to you when you were 15 or 16, and Blur were head and shoulders above any of the other bands around at that time. And always will be.

n.b. all songs written by Albarn/Coxon/James/Rowntree, all lyrics by Albarn, unless otherwise stated

CHAPTER ONE
Whitechapel, Leytonestone to Colchester, Essex – In the Beginning (1988-1990)

Before the indie-rock band Blur became the million-selling, genre-defying, cheeky Cockney-rebels that helped define nineties British guitar music, they went by a number of even less rock 'n' roll names, one of the first being, Circus. Having dropped out of his East London drama school because he didn't agree with the teaching methods, singer/songwriter Damon Albarn put Circus together with a couple of fellow dropouts in October 1988. Ironically, drama school had managed to deter Albarn from acting and pushed him straight into the evil clutches of rock 'n' roll. British music would never be the same again.

The band was designed as an outlet for the backlog of material Albarn had accumulated by this point, the other members simply providing support for his over-arching vision, and the plan was to record an album once the band were up to scratch. Damon soon drafted in a drummer he knew from back in Colchester, council worker Dave Rowntree, who at 24 was a massive five years senior to anyone else in the group; and after the initial lead guitarist dropped out, Damon put in a call to a friend from school who had also moved up to London, for university. The 18 year old Graham Coxon took to his new role with the same verve that he should have been applying to his studies, and the album was recorded in November 1988. Then after Circus played their first concert that same month, Eddie Deedigan and Dave Brolan dropped out, and Graham's friend from university was drafted in to join on bass, his name was Alex James. This was December 1989 and the band's line-up has been the same ever since.

Circus became Seymour and overnight their style of music shifted away from soul boy/rock to the band's early duelling influences of erratic post-punk and shoegazing/indie-dance, the latter much more en vogue at the time than the former. Despite Albarn's backlog of material, the Circus songs were ditched along with the name, the band choosing to start afresh instead.

Of the Circus material James said, "It was too drama college and it needed to be more art college"[i]. The new band found their way into a studio as soon as they could and the first song they wrote at their first rehearsal was also their first single, the blissed-out indie-dance track She's So High. "He [Damon] got his lyrics book and started singing 'she's so high, she's so high,'" says James in his autobiography, *Bit of a Blur*[ii]. "It all happened there and then. It was instantaneous, shockingly so…I went home for Christmas thinking 'I'm in the best band in the world.'" Graham and Alex were still in their very first term of university, predictably, neither would finish their degrees.

She's So High fit easily into the more accessible end of the shoegazing scene that was seeing the likes of Ride and My Bloody Valentine take effects-heavy soundscapes into the charts in the late eighties and early nineties, but this move was by design rather than coincidence, they knew that to make it, they would need to leave those punk roots behind.

The band began hanging around Club Syndrome on Oxford Street, where a DJ known only as Neil, would play tracks by the latest indie bands. Alongside Blur, propping up the bar on a Thursday night could be seen the likes of Lush, Ride, Chapterhouse, Slowdive and Spitfire, along with the first of Blur's arch-nemeses, Suede, and what the press love to describe as a scene, was formed. Seymour/Blur took influence from the shoegazing bands, but also had a penchant for chucking themselves around the stage, and very soon, would eclipse all of their success. The band that we know as Blur took its first hesitant step on the long road to success.

An Early Question of Class

But, let's go back a bit, where and when were they from, and how did that place inspire or conspire against them in creating their music and image? Colchester, is the simple answer. Well, three quarters of them were from the small Essex town anyway. Born in May 1964, Dave Rowntree is the ranking old timer in Blur. He grew up in Colchester and after leaving school he worked as a computer programmer for Colchester Borough Council before being plucked away by Damon to join Circus (commuting until they landed a record deal). Damon knew Dave from playing in bands around town, and Dave was taught music by Graham Coxon's father, later also playing with Graham as part of the tiny indie music scene that Colchester fostered in the late eighties.

Damon Albarn was born in March 1968, and after relocating from North London, he started at Stanway Comprehensive when he was 11 years old. A year later Graham Coxon, the youngest member of Blur, born in March 1969, also started at Stanway, having moved from Germany, where his father played in a military band. Albarn and Coxon bonded over a shared musicality, hiding from bullies in the music portacabins at lunch time, Graham playing along to Damon's piano, on his saxophone. So, just like Dave, it was no surprise when Graham also got the call to join the band that Damon was putting together in London.

Alex James, born in September 1968, was the only member of the band not from Colchester, hailing instead from the comfortable middle-class surroundings of Bournemouth on the South coast of England. He did well at school and ended up picking French to study at one of the country's leading fine art colleges, Goldsmiths. He met Graham on the very first day on campus and the pair soon began to jam not long afterwards, making him first choice when Circus needed a bass player.

There is little to say about Colchester in the late nineteen eighties other than as a mostly white, middle-class commuter town, it provided very little in the way of inspiration for the young members of Blur, other than an excuse to leave. Being just 50 miles outside of London, leaving was also relatively easy, and each of the three of them jumped on the Waterloo bound train as soon as was feasibly possible, trekking that 50 miles to the vibrant nation capital.

For Damon Albarn, moving to London was something of a return home. He had been born in Whitechapel, the heart of the East End, to hippie, struggling artist parents, moving to Leytonstone at the age of five, an area of North London made famous only by its other alumnus, the film director, Alfred Hitchcock. When he was nine the family moved out of London, like so many of their contemporaries, to the middle-class comfort of Aldham in Essex in search of a better life. His father, no longer the struggling artist, took up the incredibly bourgeois job of Head Teacher of The School of Art and Design at Colchester Institute. His mother worked behind the scenes in the theatre, mostly designing sets. In the 2003 Britpop film *Live Forever* Albarn describes the region by saying, "They had taken Thatcher's dream, and they had really gone for it…but the environment was really fucked up." In 2016, Colchester would vote to leave the EU by 53.6%, well above the final national result of 51.89%.

London on the other hand is and was a world unto itself, and the late eighties was no different. Ska-pop band Madness and the Coventry based Two Tone label had been a huge influence on the formative years of Albarn and Coxon, Damon later saying, "Madness are immensely important folk heroes in British pop music", and some of the melody lines of Blur's first two albums *Leisure* and *Modern Life is Rubbish* were heavily influenced from some of the early Madness records, alongside the other great eighties London group, The Jam.

The music was just as important as the clothes. The Doc Martin boots, and Fred Perry T-shirts of the *Modern Life* era, even earning them the moniker of "mop-top skinheads" by the NME[iii]. Madness, who had shot to fame with the excellent first album *One Step Beyond*, in 1979, hailed from Camden in North London, and it was here that Blur based themselves, Coxon still living in the borough today. Food Records too was based in Camden, and the band even signed their record contract in the Good Mixer pub, the venue that would soon become famous the world over for its prominence in the Britpop story.

The Young British Artists

Aside from Two Tone, an early part of Blur's identity was founded on their association with the art world, and in particular, the group that came to be known as the Young British Artists (YBAs), who came to prominence in the late eighties and early nineties. James' comment about Blur needing to be more art college hit the nail on its proverbial head, and the band's subsequent shift in tone began what would be an association with the art world that they would never properly manage to shake. As previously stated, Coxon and James had met studying at Goldsmiths College of Art in 1988. The pair of them were a year younger than Damien Hirst, soon to be leader of the YBAs, and soon to be one of the most successful British artists of all time. Hirst would later direct the video for Blur's Country House and be a founder member of Alex James' side-project Fat Les, who had a number 2 smash-hit in 1998 with Vindaloo.

As the nineties bore on, the UK art world became seen as more and more bourgeois and pretentious, bands like Oasis and Pulp making it trendy again to be working-class. By 1995 the art world association became to Blur's detriment, but as they were finding their feet in the late eighties, the link to the YBAs, undoubtably helped give them another of those key steps up.

UK art in the late eighties was experiencing something of a renaissance, with London the clear centre of the growing scene. The now firmly established Turner Prize was first awarded in 1984 to anyone that was pushing the boundaries of art in the UK, the likes of Richard Long, Howard Hodgkin and Gilbert & George, receiving the early awards. Then in 1991, with the emergence of youngsters such as Rachel Whiteread, Tracey Emin and Sarah Lucas (the latter two opening their famous shop, called The Shop, on Bethnal Green Road in 1993), the focus of the Turner Prize was shifted toward the up and coming rather than the established, and it was decided that the award would only go to someone under the age of 50 (this was only finally overturned in 2016), and the Young British Artist movement was born.

The development of young talent would see the Turner Prize evolve away from traditional painting and sculpture, into the world of conceptual art, Rachel Whiteread winning in 1993 with *House*, which consisted of a replication of the entirety of a three-storey London house; and then into the realms of visual art, the now hugely successful film director Steve McQueen (*Shame*, *12 years a Slave*) winning in 1999 for his film *Deadpan* (1997). The short was a take on the Buster Keaton film *Steam Boat Bill, Jr.* (1928), which includes the stunt that sees the side of house fall on a man (Keaton, and then McQueen in his remake), who is unhurt as he stands where the empty window is. Although McQueen won the award, that year's press attention was mostly centred on Tracy Emin's piece, *My Bed*. The artwork consisted simply of Emin's own bed, surrounded by all the detritus of a normal life, such as cigarette packets and condoms. It quite easily could have been the subject of a Blur song.

Whilst still in his second year at Goldsmiths in 1988, Damien Hirst had shot to fame as the creator of the

Freeze art exhibition in London's docklands. Several more high-profile exhibitions followed and then in 1992 the advertising mogul and self-confessed artoholic Charles Saatchi funded the YBA's first show at his gallery. Sarah Lucas (another Goldsmiths alumnus) and Rachel Whiteread also showed at this first exhibition.

Hirst found himself nominated for the 1992 Turner prize for his shark in formaldehyde, titled *The Physical Impossibility of Death in the Mind of Someone Living*, the iconic piece cost £50,000 to make and Saatchi would sell it in 2004 for US$8 million. Hirst would eventually win the Turner prize in 1995 – around the same time he was making headlines for directly the Country House video – this time with two dissected cows, also in formaldehyde, once again fitting thematically into Hirst's fixation with death and rebirth. The piece was wryly called *Mother and Child Divided.*

Blur aside, the closest that the art world and the music world came together in the early nineties was with the strange case of The KLF, who seemed to relish in making a mockery of everything both the art and the music worlds stood for. Despite their enormous success in the charts, The KLF saw the art and music businesses as bloated and pretentious, and decided to show them up for what they really were, with their own special brand of situationist drama. Their story can be distilled to the two most prominent things they are still remembered for: the single Justified & Ancient, which went to number 2 in December 1991; and burning £1 million, the entirety of the royalties they made, in August 1994.

Founded by sometime record exec/band manager Bill Drummond, and musician Jimi Cauty, as an outlet for Drummond's desire to create a part hip-hop, part dance group. They had their first number 1 single in June 1988 with Doctorin' the Tardis, a Doctor Who pastiche novelty record, under the name, The Timelords. This was followed with a string of hit singles under The KLF moniker, including the January 1991 number 1 single 3am Eternal, which they performed at the Brit Awards in February 1992, announcing their retirement from the music industry by firing guns into the audience at the ceremony. The guns were filled with blanks, but the retirement was real, and by May 1992, they had deleted their entire back catalogue, preventing their music from being released again ever.

A run of high-profile stunts designed to spend out the huge royalties they had amassed followed, including offering the inaugural K Foundation Award to the winner of that year's Turner Prize in 1993. Rachel Whiteread, who as previously mentioned won that year with *House*, was presented with the K Foundation Award for *worst* artist of the year. The award was for £40,000, double the Turner award, and Whiteread was forced to accept or the money was threatened with being burned.

A threat that it soon became clear Drummond and Cauty would have followed through with when the K Foundation's stunts culminated in the now infamous *The K Foundation Burn a Million Quid* episode. On 23rd August 1994, the duo elusively made their way to the Scottish island of Jura, it being illegal to destroy money of any value in the UK they had to make sure they travelled unseen, and burned the remainder of the money they had made from their record sales. The stunt was captured on an hour-long film, called *Watch the K Foundation Burn a Million Quid*, which later toured the country.

Ever the provocateurs, the pair vowed they would not speak of the event, or of The KLF, for a period of 23 years. In 2017, they hosted the three-day *Welcome to the Dark Ages* event, Drummond finally admitted regretting burning the money.

Affixing themselves with the art school connection was a conscious move by Blur as they looked to forge an identity, but it would later be used by northern rival group Oasis as a weapon, pocking a judging finger at Blur's supposed pretentious middle-class background. A fate worse than death for a pop group in 1995. There was a reason that the Melody Maker's Steve Sutherland had called shoegazing "the scene that celebrates itself," filled as it was with ex-public school boys from middle-class university towns such as Oxford, playing not to the crowds, but to each other. The sixties working-class groups such as The Beatles and The Kinks had made way for the middle-class rock groups of the seventies like Pink Floyd and Genesis, groups comprised of classically trained musicians that could afford the rows of synthesizers necessary to create the hour long LPs popular throughout the decade.

Synthesizers then took centre place throughout the eighties as pop went electronic with era-defining acts like the Pet Shop Boys and the Human League, straight indie-rock acts like The Stone Roses and the Happy Mondays using drum loops and samples to help augment their music, at the beginning of the nineties. The back to basics approach of Britpop would see the rejection of samples and synthesizers and the return of live acoustic instruments, and with it the return of working-class pride, personified in the northern charm of the Gallagher brothers.

London and Food

As 1989 bore on Seymour gathered some momentum playing at North London toilet venues as a frantic punk outfit in the vein of the late seventies British acts Buzzcocks, Undertones, The Clash, The Prefects et al, drawing attention by chucking themselves around the stage and playing intense but predominantly tuneless songs which were much more fun to play than to listen to. As Damon said at the time, "We have no intention of duplicating our live sound, the record should be something great, while live is more of an exhilarating thing."

It was the other more contemporary side of the band's sound, the She's So High side, that they would soon put on record, that Andy Ross, joint head of the indie label Food Records, was drawn to when he turned up to see one of these gigs in November 1989. Ross heard a demo of She's So High and after seeing them play was drawn to Albarn's looks and the fact that you couldn't take your eyes of him or them on stage. Ross returned a few more times, and then the band signed to Food in February 1990, She's So High being released as their first single in October that same year. Ross' one proviso was that they change their name (and that Dave Rowntree not be allowed to wear his pyjama bottoms on stage).

And Seymour/Blur's route to the charts really was that simple. They had no following or fanbase to speak of and had to work hard once they had landed their deal to gain one. This was done the old-fashioned way by touring touring touring. But that's how things worked back then, an A&R guy would take a punt on a group he liked the look of and then stick with them, working on intuition alone. Sometimes it would work, most of the time it didn't, but it was never contrived.

After the best part of a year of constant touring it was October 1990, just as their first single was due for release, that things finally started to fall into place. On Friday 26th October 1990 they played at JBs in Dudley near Birmingham, far away from their native London turf. As Alex James says, "Of all the shows we've ever played, that was the most memorable. They just got it, right there and then."[iv] Things were starting to come together.

Signing their Life Away

Back in the Circus days Damon had signed a management contract with The Beat Factory, run by ex-musicians Graeme Holdaway and Marijke Bergkamp, who gave the fledgling musician free recording time in the studio that they ran. It was Bergkamp that booked Seymour's gigs and who gave the demo tape to Andy Ross, but by the end of 1989 the management contract was due for renewal and Albarn decided against continuing the relationship, choosing instead to go all in with their new record company. This may have seemed like something of a blow to Holdaway and Bergkamp, but in some minor form of recompense, Blur would include some of the material recorded at this time on the B-sides to their seventh single, October 1993's Sunday Sunday. Tell Me, Tell Me; Dizzy; Fried; Long Legged and Shimmer were all credited to Graeme Holdaway as producer. Never too far away from their Seymour roots, Blur later dug up Fried, playing it live whilst at the peak of their success.

Had they kept Beat Factory's council then they may well have had the foresight to ask for a slightly better deal than the steal of the century that Ross and his partner Dave Balfe paid, a paltry £3,000 advance (£6,250 in today's money).

Not that they had the money to pay them much more though. Balfe, originally from Liverpool, had formed his first label Zoo with one Bill Drummond, from The KLF, in order to release the first single by Echo & the Bunnymen in 1978. That art world connection once again. He then founded the tiny indie label Food in 1984, but only in April 1990 would they experience their first top 20 single with Jesus Jones' Real Real Real, not long after the newly christened Blur had signed their contract. Jesus Jones' second album *Doubt* would then go to number 1 in February 1991. Most importantly though, Real Real Real went to number 4 in the US Billboard Top 100, its follow up Right Here, Right Now reaching number 2 in September 1990 (number 1 in the Billboard Modern Rock Tracks chart), which of course was where the money was.

This success bought in the funds to help develop the new signing, and the smallness of the label meant that Blur had Dave and Andy's absolute attention, affording them the opportunity of developing at their own pace. Which as we'll come to see, gave Blur the lifeline they would need to come back from near death, not once, but twice.

Before that though, it was time for the release of their first single.

Single 1:

She's So High
Released: 15th October 1990; UK Chart Position: 48*; Label: Food; Album: *Leisure*
B-sides: I Know; Down

*the single reached its highest position on its second week of release

UK Official Singles Chart – Top 10 – 28th October 1990:

1. Unchained Melody (1990) – The Righteous Brothers
2. A Little Time – The Beautiful South
3. Take My Breath Away (1990) – Berlin
4. Show Me Heaven – Tina McKee
5. I'm Your Baby Tonight – Whitney Houston
6. (We Want) The Same Thing – Belinda Carlisle
7. Kinky Afro – Happy Mondays
8. The Anniversary Waltz – Part One – Status Quo
9. Step Back in Time – Kylie Minogue
10. Blue Velvet – Bobby Vinton

....

45. She's so High – Blur

Blur's first single was released into a chart dominated by slow-paced ballads sung by female belters.

And the Happy Mondays. Both Unchained Melody and Take My Breath Away had existing chart history, and had been rereleased because of their inclusion on film soundtracks: the former famed for its use in the pottery wheel scene in *Ghost* (1990), and the latter from *Top Gun* (1986), here rereleased because of the film's first showing on television, such was the power of the medium at the time. Also present were some younger singers who had made their name ten years earlier, Belinda Carlisle, Kylie and Whitney Houston, showing that in 1990, the eighties were far from over.

The alternative scene though was represented in the form of the Happy Mondays, who were enjoying their second top 10 single with Kinky Afro, showing just how popular the Madchester scene was at this time. At the beginning of the new decade, bands from London were mostly out of vogue in favour of their northern compatriots from Manchester, and the Haçienda, run by Factory Records, was one of the world's most famous nightclubs. The Madchester scene was led predominantly by The Stone Roses and the Happy Mondays, who despite having something of a similar aesthetic had binary opposed temperaments, the former taking the production of their music incredibly seriously, whilst the latter, well, not so much, focusing more on the hedonism that ran concurrent to the scene.

Then after the so called Second-Summer-of-Love in 1988, where the crowds who had been drawn by the ecstasy had stayed for the music, Acid House crossed over into the mainstream, bringing indie-rock with it.

Both the Mondays and the Roses found their success reach new heights with remixes by up-and-coming DJs (Paul Oakenfold's legendary remix of the Mondays' Hallelujah helped take the Madchester EP into the top 20 in November 1989), or by merging the two styles together, employing elements from Acid House such as drum loops and overly long repeated instrumentals, marrying them with traditional guitar riffs and minimalist and often non-sensical lyrics (what exactly is a kinky afro?). By July 1990 The Stone Roses would notch up three top 10 singles in a row, before sadly disappearing for four years amongst a hailstorm of a fall out with their record company.

On advice of Food and their new producer Stephen Street – who had had his finger on the pulse since he engineered for The Smiths five years previously – Blur followed suit and the result was their second single and first pop masterpiece, April 1991's There's No Other Way, a song noted for its classic indie guitar lick, set against a hip-hop cribbed drum loop.

Six months later Nirvana would release *Nevermind* and everything would change.

CHAPTER TWO
There's No Other Way and *Leisure* – Blur Begins (1991)

Blur's relationship with Stephen Street was their most important one outside of the four members of the band, Andy Ross and Dave Balfe included. Street would helm their musical direction through the beginning stages of Britpop with *Modern Life is Rubbish* in 1993, the monumental highs of success with *Parklife* in 1994, the falling fortunes of *The Great Escape* in 1995, and it was he that made their change of direction possible with their eponymous album in 1997. Probably most importantly, it was with him at the mixing desk when they created their first bona fide hit single, There's No Other Way in 1991. It's just a shame he wasn't around to help out with their debut album *Leisure*, later that same year.

"I did five albums with the band [he includes his contributions to *Leisure*]," said Street to *Sound on Sound*, after he was not asked to produce their sixth album *13* in 1999[v], "and I must admit I thought each one would be the last because they were bound to want to try something new."

Each of Blur's albums is vastly different from the previous one, much more so than any of their contemporaries, apart from perhaps Radiohead, and this was aided by their continued decision to work with Street. This made the decision to move away from him with *13* seem even stranger, despite Street's own lack of surprise. On being asked to leave the band in 2003, whilst they were recording *Think Tank*, Graham Coxon turned to Street to produce his third solo album, the top 20 hit *Happiness in Magazines*, by far his most successful solo effort. Then, when the band reformed and decided to record another album in 2014, Street was the first choice for Blur mark 3.0 to produce *The Magic Whip*.

Of course, how fruitful Street's relationship with Blur would become wasn't known back in 1991, and he applied for the job of Blur producer after hearing She's So High on the radio. Chief among his credentials at the time was having engineered and produced The Smiths albums, as well as co-writing Morrissey's classic 1988 solo album, *Viva Hate*. Damon Albarn had previously said, "What made me want to be in a band was seeing a South Bank Show on The Smiths and hearing Morrissey say that pop music was dead, and that The Smiths had been the last group of any significance. I remember thinking, 'No-one is going to tell me that pop music is finished.'" Who better to help him reinvent pop music than the man who helped Morrissey kill it.

Things got off to a solid start, with the immediate success of There's No Other Way in April 1991. Despite the band's claims to the contrary ("Baggy is Northern, we're from London") the track could have been one of the lead tracks on 'Best Baggy Hits, 1991', had that existed.

Street followed the many examples (EMF, KLF, Wonder Stuff et al) of lifting a hip-hop drum beat and layering a jangly guitar line on the top. Coxon's riff, which would draw a huge cry of "yeah…!" every time it was played on an indie club dance floor over the next twenty years, sounded like the sixties by way of the nineties, before the nineties had even properly got going, and the song quickly became an anthem, reaching number 8 in the charts in April 1991.

Single 2:

There's No Other Way
Released: 15th April 1991; UK Chart Position: 8*; Label: Food; Album: *Leisure*
B-sides: Inertia; Mr Briggs; I'm All Over

*the single reached its highest position on week four of its release

UK Official Singles Chart – Top 10 – 12th May 1991:

1. The Shoop Shoop Song (It's in His Kiss) – Cher
2. Last Train to Trancentral – KLF ft. The Children of the Revolution
3. Gypsy Woman (La Da Dee) – Crystal Waters
4. Sailing in the Seven Seas – Orchestral Manoeuvres in the Dark
5. Touch Me (All Night Long) – Cathy Dennis
6. Promise Me – Beverley Craven
7. Senza Una Donna (Without a Woman) – Zucchero ft. Paul Young
8. **There's No Other Way – Blur**
9. Get the Message – Electronic
10. Tainted Love – Soft Cell ft. Marc Almond

The chart that Blur's first top 10 single was released into was very similar to the one that their first single was six months earlier. Number 1 was yet another song from a film, this time, another family favourite *Mermaids* (1990), staring Cher, who also sang the theme song. Also, behind Blur was another Madchester act, this time in the slightly more sophisticated guise of Electronic and their second single Get the Message. Electronic was the supergroup comprised of New Order's Bernard Sumner and Johnny Marr from The Smiths.

In its first week of release There's No Other Way reached a not disrespectable number 20, a position that earned them a spot on Britain's premier music TV show *Top of the Pops.* Despite its reputation for bubble-gum pop,

TOTP was still the Holy Grail for all indie bands because it meant you had crossed over into the mainstream, and in the case of Blur, your single could be pushed up into the top 10 the following week.

At Blur's 1999 Reading Festival headline slot Damon admitted to the 50,000 strong crowd that he and Alex had been given an ecstasy pill before the performance. It certainly shows in Damon's loved-up performance, and in the fact that the strings on Alex's bass had been undone. Coxon had been late to the performance and nearly didn't make it into the studio at all after an argument with the security guard, meaning that he missed out on the pill that made Damon and Alex's performances so engaging. Well, the early bird catches the worm.

Single 3:

Bang
Released: 29th July 1991; UK Chart Position: 24*;
Label: Food; Album: *Leisure*
B-sides: Explain; Luminous; Berserk

*the single reached its highest position on its second week of release

With There's No Other Way having pushed the band out there into the world, the time was right for their debut album, but the record company thought they needed to release one more single first, and despite the band's protestations, Bang was released in July 1991. During the band's 1999 singles tour, when they played each of their singles in order of release, Damon made it quite clear that Bang was his least favourite Blur song.

The song is listenable enough and follows closely in the footsteps of the band's previous two singles, with a jangly Byrds-esque guitar riff, and a chorus of "I don't need anyone, but a little love will make things better" didn't sound out of place on the radio. It would be their last baggy style release and their last single until Popscene in March 1992 changed everything.

UK Official Singles Chart – Top 10 – 11th August 1991:

1. (Everything I Do) I Do It For You – Bryan Adams
2. I'm Too Sexy – Right Said Fred
3. More Than Words – Extreme
4. Move Any Mountain – The Shamen
5. Set Adrift on Memory Bliss – PM Dawn
6. All 4 One – Color Me Badd
7. Winter in July – Bomb the Bass
8. Now That We've Found Love – Heavy D and the Boys
9. Enter Sandman – Metallica
10. Summertime – DJ Jazzy Jeff and the Fresh Prince

....

24. Bang – Blur

One guess what was at number 1 when Bang first charted. That's right, a song from a film soundtrack. This time it also happened to be the song that had the longest ever run at the top spot, Canadian rocker Bryan Adams' (Everything I Do) I Do It For You, taken from the Kevin Costner-tastic classic *Robin Hood: Prince of Thieves* (1991). The single enjoyed a mind-numbing sixteen weeks at the top spot before it was toppled by U2's The Fly. Three years later Wet Wet Wet would equal Adams' feat with their version of Love is All Around Me, yet again, a song from a film, this time *Four Weddings and a Funeral* (1994), which was for a long while the most successful British film of all time.

Leisure – Debut Album

<u>Album 1:</u>

Leisure
Released: 26th August 1991; UK Chart Position: 7; Label: Food
Track Listing: She's So High; Bang; Slow Down; Repetition; Bad Day; Sing; There's No Other Way; Fool; Come Together; High Cool; Birthday; Wear Me Down
Producer/s: Steve Lovell, Steve Power, Mike Thorne, Stephen Street

All too often, a band's debut album is the best one that they will release. Having spent the first twenty-something years of their life stock piling songs, it makes sense. The examples are many: The Smiths, *The Smiths*; Joy Division, *Unknown Pleasures*; The Stone Roses, *The Stone Roses*; PJ Harvey, *Dry*; Oasis, *Definitely Maybe*; Elastica, *Elastica*; and then more recently The Libertines, *Up the Bracket*; Arctic Monkeys, *Whatever People Say I Am, That's What I'm Not*; The Black Rebel Motorcycle Club, *BRMC*; The Strokes, *Is this It?*

Some of these, but by no means all of them, manage to continue the trend with a second album that is just as good as the first: The Smiths, *Meat is Murder*; Arctic Monkeys, *Favourite Worst Nightmare*; The Libertines, *The Libertines*; and some that far outstrip the achievements and the performance of the first: Oasis, *(What's the Story) Morning Glory?*; Nirvana, *Nevermind*; Amy Winehouse, *Back to Black*; Daft Punk, *Discovery*; Adele, *21*.

And then there are some bands that have a debut album so out of synch with the sound that they finally manage to create that listeners discovering the band years later are amazed that it is the same band at all. Radiohead are in this bracket, as are Blur.

Leisure is far from the disaster of an album that many often consider it to be. It is though, a messy album. It is with hindsight we can say that Stephen Street should have helmed the whole record, but it is amazing that he managed to produce the tracks that he did, having had an unspecified falling out with Dave Balfe around this time. Instead, the mixing desk chair passed between Street, Steve Lovell, Steve Power and the only one of the four not called Steve, Mike Thorne. If you add in the fact that the album was recorded in two different studios and in small snippets of time, rather than in one go, the result is a schizophrenic collection of songs crossing a range of genres: baggy, punk, indie-rock and grunge, despite the fact the band's claims to hate the latter genre.

Lyrically, it is with the band's next album, *Modern Life is Rubbish*, that Damon began his slice-of-life look at fish-and-chip culture, telling stories through his songs, but there are glimpses of it in some of the material around this time. Mr Briggs, the B-side to There's No Other Way is a Kinks song if Jimi Hendrix's had played lead guitar, and tells the story of the titular character, who could have joined the cast of *Parklife*: "Mr Briggs is on holiday, But he stays in his room, He's too cold to go out for his evening smoke."

Bang also uses this tactic, for all of Damon's claims to hate the song, the subject matter is not too dissimilar to For Tomorrow, opening track on *Modern Life…* beginning with the line, "Sitting in a SDT, Waiting for an underground train, To rumble underneath my feet." On the whole though, the stories are missing from *Leisure*, the songs seemingly not about much at all. Which to be fair to the group, was how most of their contemporary groups worked at the time. The Wonder Stuff's most famous song, for example, ran with the key line "building up your problem to the size of a cow".

Tonally the band skip through their influences on the album, flinging a range of musical styles at it, in the vein hope that something will stick. On Slow Down and Repetition, Albarn lifts the melodies and close harmonies from the first two Madness albums, whilst Graham Coxon plays guitar lines underneath that wouldn't have sounded out of place at the local grunge night; and the whole second half of the record sounds like it was recorded by a second tier band signed to Creation Records circa 1987. The opening line of at least two of the songs is, "I don't understand". Which perhaps says it all. It is not that the album is bad, it is just mostly direction-less, which sat at total odds with the band's spewed rhetoric about how they hated everything else around at the time.

The album's stand out track, The Happy Mondays meets Ride indie-dance crossover There's No Other Way, worked because the track fit seamlessly in with the zeitgeist, whilst maintaining its own identity, and sounded good being blasted from the speakers of student bedrooms. The problem was though that none of the other songs on the album follow its example.

Aside from She's So High and There's No Other Way, only Sing – written on the battered piano in Damon's mother's art studio when the band were staying over on one of their earliest tours – shows promise of what the band could be. Consisting of the crashing staccato piano, the looped snare drum and the dirty-angelic chorus 'ahhs', the song is an atmospheric epic, reminiscent of early Bowie and Lou Reed, but because of its subtlety it was overlooked at the time of release. Film director Danny Boyle picked it out of near forgotten obscurity, adding it to the sequence where things fall apart for Ewan MacGregor's Mark Renton in the drug-fuelled incendiary 1996 hit film *Trainspotting*, and the song was finally secured the position that it deserved.

The somewhat confused, but not completely unlistenable album reached a not disrespectful number 7 in the charts when it was released in August 1991, eventually shifting 150,000 copies and going gold, but failed to set the world on fire as many had predicted.

UK Official Albums Chart – Top 10 – 1st September 1991:

1. *Joseph and his Amazing Technicolour Dreamcoat* – Jason Donovan and the London Cast
2. *Love Hurts* – Cher
3. *CMB* – Color Me Badd
4. *Seal* – Seal
5. *Out of Time* – R.E.M.
6. *Essential Pavarotti II* – Luciano Pavarotti
7. ***Leisure* – Blur**
8. *The Immaculate Collection* – Madonna
9. *Sugar Tax* – Orchestral Manoeuvres in the Dark
10. *Fellow Hoodlums* – Deacon Blue

Just a quick glance at the albums chart in September 1991 tells you that it was something of an achievement for Blur to get as high as number 7 that week. With the cast of a West End musical claiming the top spot, and opera singer Pavarotti one place higher, it seemed that the record buying public was looking the other way. As something in the way of evening the score, Oasis' debut album *Definitely Maybe* would top the charts over Pavarotti three years later in August 1994. But in 1991, that was still a long way off.

Knowing they were capable of much more, the band were unsure quite what to do next. They survived this strange period by continually touring and relying on the crowds that flocked to see Albarn throw himself around the stage whilst they tried to work out what type of band they were.

Whilst they were busy finding themselves America invaded Britain when it wasn't looking and grunge and its leaders Nirvana became the hottest ticket on both sides of the Atlantic. Love was out and hating yourself was in, a paradigm shift that killed off the Happy Mondays in its wake and left The Stone Roses in exile for four years. The Hacienda traipsed on but was soon abandoned by the kids, who were busy injecting heroin instead of ingesting ecstasy, and listening to Mudhoney and Soundgarden.

Grunge seemed to come from nowhere, surprising even its native America, as much as it did the UK and the rest of the world. Just as we later saw with Britpop, the scene rose from an underground independent movement (centred nominally around Seattle), and originally began as a reaction to groups and individuals' displeasure with their lot in life. Just like punk did in the late seventies, disenfranchised youths turned to music to help them release the pent-up aggression and frustration back at the society that they perceived was treating them unfairly. Kurt Cobain, perhaps the pinnacle of grunge, proved himself to be both an incredibly gifted songwriter, perhaps one of the best since Lennon and McCartney, directly in touch with the feelings of the youth at the time. With songs like Lithium, which took its name from an anti-depressant that can leave the taker numbed to their surroundings, and later Rape Me, on which he sang about his feelings of how the commercialisation of his music was destroying him, he tried again and again to forge his own pathway, and fight back against the system. Eventually, he gave up, tragically taking his own life in April 1994.

Totally at odds with the love-in of what was going on in Manchester and around the UK with the club culture in the late eighties and early nineties, grunge completely took over, destroying the idea of peace and freedom in its wake. People were angry again, and with Nirvana's *Nevermind* spending a mammoth 346 weeks on the UK Official Albums Chart, most recently in the top 100 at the beginning of October 2020, it seemed that there was no place for Blur left in Britain. Their next move, whatever it was, would need to be the best one yet.

CHAPTER THREE
Modern Life Is Rubbish – Blur Define the Popscene – Britpop Now (1992-93)

Despite the drastic shift in focus toward grunge in 1991, Blur released the very British stand-alone single Popscene on 30th March 1992. With its hypnotic bass riff and phaser guitar line, not to mention the glorious stampede of its brass refrain, the song had captured audiences' attentions ever since they had first played it live in late 1991. Little did the band, their record company, or their audience know that with this single they were about to invent what would become Britain's next major musical movement, that would ultimately help to define the nineties, in just the way that grunge defined the nineties in the States.

Popscene sat somewhere between all of the musical worlds the band had previously explored, the pace of a punk track married with the layered guitar lines of the best bits of *Leisure*, whilst appearing as fresh as a cool breeze on the over-indulged warmed corpse that grunge would soon become.

The band and their record company thought the song was fantastic. The record buying public disagreed and the single stalled at number 32 in the charts. "[Popscene is] just a directionless organ-fest in search of a good chorus," said Melody Maker. However, "It was Nirvana that really fucked Popscene up," countered Graham Coxon.

Single 4:

Popscene
Released: 30th March 1992; UK Chart Position: 32;
Label: Food; Album: n/a
B-sides: Mace; Badgeman Brown
Producer: Steve Lovell

UK Official Singles Chart – Top 10 – 5th April 1992:

1. Stay – Shakespeare's Sister
2. Deeply Dippy – Right Said Fred
3. To Be With You – Mr Big
4. Joy – Soul II Soul
5. Why – Annie Lennox
6. Finally (1992) – Ce Ce Peniston
7. Let's Get Rocked – Def Leppard
8. Save the Best for Last – Vanessa Williams
9. (I Want to Be) Elected – Mr Bean and the Smear Campaign
10. Evapor 8 – Altern 8

....

32. Popscene – Blur

Popscene had originally been intended as the first single from Blur's second album, and another track that nearly didn't see the light of day, Never Clever, was even slated for release as the follow up single, but plans for both the single and the album were ditched after Popscene's weak chart placing. Never Clever eventually surfaced as one of the many B-sides to Chemical World, in July 1993.

Despite the single's relatively poor performance in the charts, Food remained loyal to their young wards and where other bands may have found themselves dropped after the flop, they knew they were capable of more. The audience's muted reaction to Popscene gave them pause for thought though, and so instead of recording what would have been their second album, they were forced onto a tour to pay off their mounting debts.

Leisure had made its money back, and then some, so there should have been money in the bank, some £400,000 to be exact. So why wasn't there? The band parted ways with their first manager Mike Collins around this time, and Collins' face is blanked out in the 1993 documentary *Starshaped*, so the fingers were certainly pointing one way. The band were left some £100,000 in debt. With a new manager on board, the veteran Chris Morrison, the shell-shocked group were forced onto a lengthy tour of – suitably enough – America, and were away for the middle of 1992, a year that had certainly not started out as well for them as 1991 had.

When they returned to London, beleaguered, with month long hang overs, the plan was to begin recording their new album. This they set to with Andy Partridge from eighties new wavers XTC at the helm. They put down Sunday Sunday and Coping, and a few others, before abandoning the whole thing, feeling that the relationship wasn't working. Damon's strong personality clashed with Partridge's draconian style of producing and it was only after a strong word from his girlfriend Justine Frischmann (more on her later), that Damon began to realise the band were never going to emerge from their self-created despair hole if he didn't pull his head out of his own behind and start leading again.

Still with Food's support, the band returned once more to the studio, this time to Fulham's Rouge Mansion (where they had recorded There's No Other Way), and finally with Stephen Street at the helm. Coxon had bumped into Street at a Cranberries concert (he had produced their first album, the mega-hit *Everybody else is Doing it, So Why Can't We?* due out in March 1993), and their conversation encouraged Street to revisit his relationship with Blur. The album was begun proper at the beginning of September 1992, and they finished in time for the Christmas break on 16th December. Or so they thought. Dave Balfe thought that the album was missing an obvious single, so Damon's Christmas homework was to write one. This he did, hung over and dejected on Christmas day 1992. What he came up with eventually turned out to be something of a turning point for the band, although it took time to percolate, only coming into its own some months after its initial release. Which was somewhat apt, considering it was called For Tomorrow.

The reaction to Popscene may have left Albarn feeling momentarily out of step with the record buying public, but the world's obsession with grunge gave him and his comrades something to fight against, and during the long tour of forgotten American music festivals, Damon's creative mind turned frequently to home. He decided what the people of Britain wanted to listen to; what they were missing amidst the considerable weight of imported grunge, was music about Britain, or British pop music, or Britpop, as it was eventually coined by one canny journalist looking for a scoop and finding one. Chew on that Morrissey!

The Beginnings of Britpop

With *Modern Life is Rubbish* in the can, Albarn's idea of British pop music was gathering some momentum. However, as it turned out, it wasn't Blur that were leading the charge. Britpop may have been "100% Damon Albarn's idea", as Alex James had it, but it was the semi-androgynous Bowie-lite fellow Londoners Suede who the press had placed at the forefront of the movement, a band who had something of a shared history with Albarn and co.

If Blur had beaten Suede to the punch by scoring themselves a hit single first, then Suede found their revenge with the release of their debut album, and by early 1993 the band quickly dominated both the headlines and the gig slots that Albarn had anticipated Blur would fill. After its catchy suggestive single (and its highly provocative video) Animal Nitrate had reached number 7 in March 1993, Suede's eponymous album went straight in at the top spot in early April, wrenching the focus away from grunge and back toward Britain and a new slew of bands focused on home culture. Unbeknownst to them, and despite their repeated reservations about both Britain and British pop music, Suede were the first to ride the Union Jack styled wave that would last for the next five years.

<u>Single 5:</u>

For Tomorrow
Released: 19th April 1993; UK Chart Position: 28;
Label: Food; Album: *Modern Life is Rubbish*
B-sides: Peach; Bone Bag
Producer: Stephen Street

Blur released their excellent new single For Tomorrow two weeks after Suede's album hit the top spot. Frustratingly, it too stalled in the charts just as its predecessor had over a year earlier, just about denting the top 30.

Considering its composition, there is a poignant, melancholic fragility to For Tomorrow. The song conjures up the very image of the contemporary London that Albarn had been aiming for and began the social commentary that would soon make him famous the world over. The first line runs, "He's a twentieth century boy", managing to both root the song in the present as well as drawing intertextual reference to the past, by employing the use of a song title by the seventies glam-rock band T-Rex, and their 1973 number 3 single 20th Century Boy.

The song goes on to use iconography specific to the capital: "London ice cracks on a seamless line", a banal yet evocative reference to winter frost on London's train lines causing delays; before switching the action to "a twentieth century girl" – perhaps the romantic interest of the first character – whose car is lost on the West Way, the A-road that runs through Notting Hill and much of West London. The song was about the now, and through drawing a picture of contemporary London, listeners could identify with the twentieth century boy and girl at the centre of the song. You add in a "la la la lala" singalong chorus, and what's not to like?

Damon even offers a half rap, half spoken word coda, layered over the top of the outro that foreshadows the similar spoken word verses to Parklife ("know what I mean?"). The lyric follows Jim, who gets out of his car at Emperor's Gate, and says "Modern Life, well, it's rubbish". He meets Susan and takes a drive to Primrose Hill, a few more carefully chosen London locations thrown in for good measure. Despite its relatively low showing in the charts, as we'll come to see, the song would eventually provide a marked turning point for the band, and is a live favourite to date.

UK Official Singles Chart – Top 10 – 25th April 1993:

1. Five Live (EP) – George Michael and Queen with Lisa Stansfield
2. Young at Heart (1993) – The Bluebells
3. I Have Nothing – Whitney Houston
4. Ain't No Love (Ain't No Use) – Sub Sub ft. Melanie Williams
5. Informer – Snow
6. U Got 2 Know – Cappella
7. When I'm Good and Ready – Sybil
8. Regret – New Order
9. Everybody Hurts – REM
10. Show Me Love – Robin S

…………………………

28. For Tomorrow – Blur

George Michael and Queen were at number 1 the week that For Tomorrow first charted, a year after their joint performance at the Freddie Mercury Tribute concert at Wembley Stadium in April 1992, with five tracks from the concert, including Somebody To Love and Those Were the Days of Our Lives, the latter performed with Lisa Stansfield.

Plus, we can see also see the continued influence of Madchester and the Haçienda with New Order at number 8 with Regret and Sub Sub at number 4 with Ain't No Love (Ain't No Use). Sub Sub would later reinvent themselves as Doves, having a string of hits as part of the new Manchester wave at the beginning of the 2000s.

Difficult Second Album Syndrome

Album 2:

Modern Life is Rubbish
Released: 10th May 1993; UK Chart Position: 15; Label: Food
Track Listing: For Tomorrow; Advert; Collin Zeal; Pressure on Julian; Star Shaped; Blue Jeans; Chemical World; (Intermission); Sunday Sunday; Oily Water; Miss America; Villa Rosie; Copying; Turn it Up; Resigned; (Commercial Break)
Producer: Stephen Street

Whether Albarn and co were ahead of themselves or the tunes still weren't strong enough, Blur's second album *Modern Life is Rubbish* also stalled in the charts, peaking at a not excellent number 15 at the end of May 1993. Which presumably drew out not a small amount of schadenfreude from Suede's lead singer Brett Anderson, who was busy being one of the biggest indie-pop stars in Britain.

Back in 1991 when Blur had cruised into the top 10 with There's No Other Way, Suede had been a struggling indie group playing the UCL students union and the Kentish Town Bull and Gate to a range of nonplussed

A&R men looking for the next Nirvana. It was around this time that Suede's rhythm guitarist and future Elastica front-woman Justin Frischmann left her current boyfriend Brett Anderson, soon coupling up with her new boyfriend Damon Albarn.

She hung around the Suede rehearsal room just long enough to regale the band members with stories about Blur video shoots and launch parties and then Brett asked her to leave, a move that culminated in him doubling down on his own creativity and so forcing the band's success by pure will power (and of course, a modicum of talent).

There is nothing like a bit of emotional turmoil to fuel creativity…

She's Not Dead, from *Suede* (1993)

She'll come to her end
Locked in a car somewhere
With exhaust in her hair
What's she called?
I don't know
She's fucking with a slip of a man
While the engine ran

The animosity between the two groups and their domineering lead singers was far more pronounced and longer lasting than that between Blur and Oasis, and just like this far more famous feud, they often traded blows in the musical press, Frischmann caught between the two camps. Albarn particularly seemed to revel in the hostility and continued his antagonism long after Anderson had stopped responding. "Damon was a real bully," said Frischmann to John Harris in *The Last Party*, "and he had a real problem with Brett, even though Brett hadn't done anything wrong as far as I could see. But they both seemed to get fired up by the fighting."

It was into this changing environment that Blur released their second album *Modern Life is Rubbish* into.

UK Official Albums Chart – Top 10 – 16th May 1993:

1. *Automatic for the People* – REM
2. *No Limits* – 2 Unlimited
3. *Republic* – New Order
4. *On the Night* – Dire Straits
5. *Home Movies – The Best of* – Everything but the Girl
6. *Ten Summoner's Tales* – Sting
7. *Banba* – Clannad
8. *Blues Alive* – Gary Moore
9. *Breathless* – Kenny G
10. *So Close* – Dina Carroll

....

15. *Modern Life if Rubbish* – Blur

A quick look at the albums chart in mid-May 1993 tells us how safe popular music was in the early nineties. REM's middle-of-the-road mega-hit album *Automatic for the People* was number 1 for the fourth non-consecutive time after 33 weeks on release; the pre-Aqua dance-pop stylings of 2 Unlimited were at number 2; and a return to form, but also decidedly radio-friendly New Order were at number 3 (down from 1) with *Republic.*

Just above Blur at 13 was Morrissey's long forgotten *Beethoven was Deaf* album, and the likes of Cliff Richard were rubbing shoulders with such disparate acts as Bon Jovi, Eric Clapton and Rage Against the Machine. The charts were in need of some focus, something that *Modern Life* would bring, if not quite the way that Damon and co. might have anticipated.

Modern Life is Rubbish

Modern Life is Rubbish is a proficient album by any standards, it is more consistent than *Leisure*, the overall themes of modern life being… well, rubbish, draw together the tracks as something of a concept album, not unlike *The Kinks are the Village Green Preservation Society*, a comparison that would not have been lost on the band.

Albarn's lyrics had developed away from the non-sensical meaninglessness so prominent in early nineties British indie music, into the observational style he would soon become famed for. The band's songs began to tell stories, and this gave them an angle, whilst deliberately steering them away from association with the blasé vapidity of other contemporary indie-groups such as The Wonder Stuff, The Farm or EMF. After experiencing some short-lived success in the early nineties, these bands were struggling to find attention as the back-to-basics nature of Britpop exposed any element of a band's sound that could be lacking. It became no longer acceptable to hide behind drum loops and samples. "Look up your sequencers!" challenged Liam Gallagher in 1994.

Interestingly *Modern Life* was the Blur album destined to become the retrospective favourite of fans, but only after the band had produced their more successful work. It is one of those albums that folk refer to when they say, "I prefer their earlier stuff". In 2013, the NME voted it the 33rd best album of all time,[vi] meaning that it has had the longevity that *Leisure* didn't quite manage.

There are many high points: the catchy pop stylings of the often overlooked Chemical World, the simplistic punk hymn to consumerism Advert ("Food processors are great!"), and Star Shaped, one of the strongest tracks to be recorded immediately post-*Leisure*, and which signalled the new direction for the band; but overall, at the time, there was the feeling that the album fell short of its mark. A feeling shared by the record buying public.

So, was the message too subtle? At that point, Britpop was being spearheaded by Suede, who were anything but subtle, and whose whole existence was predated on challenging perceived societal norms, particularly their constructed image (borrowed from Bowie) of sexual fluidity. One of Brett Anderson's famous early quotes was that he was a "a bisexual man who never had a homosexual experience". A quote that reeks of self-aggrandising more than claiming a sense of sexual identity. Whatever the intention, it worked, and it was Brett on the front cover of Select magazine in April 1993 under the headline "Yanks Go Home!" This headline, now considered to be the first to acknowledge the bourgeoning Britpop scene, joined Suede with Pulp, The Auteurs, St Etienne and even the flash-in-the-pan outfit Denim (no, me neither…), Blur not even getting a look in.

Blur's Doc Martin boots, Fred Perry t-shirts, turned up jeans and Graham's NHS specs (all carefully adorned in much of the marketing material for the album, including an oil painting on the inside sleeve), drew on iconography employed by the Two Tone bands of the eighties, as well as Mr Pop-music himself, Morrissey. The intention was to pull together the existing wealth of recent British pop history to celebrate British pop itself, but a song about a prostitute being forced to relocate to the country for her health (Chemical World) – just like the aforementioned clothing – meant that much of the actual material missed its mark due in no small part to its subtlety.

And that feeling permeates across the album, meaning that the album's real message was lost, or didn't quite make sense, until after *Parklife* had been released, over a year later. Once *Parklife* was out and doing its thing, fans were afforded the opportunity of diving back into *Modern Life* to work out how the story fell together. This meant that Colin Zeal's pleasure at being on time (yet again) made much more sense now it was in context. The lyrics tell stories, but they are mostly about frustration, lack of fulfilment and dissatisfaction. As the NME had it in their original review, "It's the Village Green Preservation Society come home to find a car park in its place."[vii] Britain was long gone from the idyll of the sixties and there was no way back.

This was perhaps not so true of the final single and centre piece of the album though, Sunday Sunday, with its brass backing, staccato guitars, overt references to walks in the park and reading the colour supplement, the track aims at being as quintessentially English as a roast dinner. Therefore, feeding into the schizophrenic nature of the album: the second half letting down the whole. With fourteen tracks, three of them should probably have been saved for B-sides. Oily Water and Miss America are passable enough, but Villa Rosie and Coping are typically Coxon-esque punky-chord led tracks reminiscent of the second half of *Leisure* (and of grunge), and which seemed to undermine the band's message about British music and Britishness. Going on much of the material alone, it wasn't exactly clear what music about Britishness looked like.

The title itself is a sly reference to how everything worthwhile has already been done (a feeling shared by each passing generation), and harks back to a more blissfully remembered foregone era, undoubtably the sixties and seventies, when the charts were filled with compositions by British songwriters such as Lennon and McCartney, Ray Davies, Steve Marriott, David Bowie and Mark Bolan, rather than Americans such as Kurt Cobain and Billy Corgon. From the position of today, this may seem like a well-trodden move, but back in 1993 retrospectively applauding the world of the sixties was not as commonplace. Each successive decade had spent its time trying to distance itself from the last, and so claim the ground for something new, rather than look at the modern time through the prism of retrospect. Albarn's idea was to build on what had been started thirty years earlier to help tell the contemporary story.

The material on *Modern Life is Rubbish* was mostly glossed over because the album became so bogged down by the weight of its own meaning. Albarn's mantra in the music press was to hammer home how his band and his music was all about an inherent Britishness. Other than singing in a cockney accent and telling tales of quintessential British characters such as Colin Zeal, "He's a pedestrian walker, he's a civil talker, He's an affable man with a plausible plan," a character who could not exist outside of Middle England, this message comes across in an inconsistent and incoherent manner over the whole album.

That said, what was there, was more than enough for any journalist looking for a reaction to grunge, which became tired and tepid almost as soon as it was brought to prominence, and so the album was weighted with a level of expectation before release. Whether it delivered on that though, the jury is still out, but what it did do, was swing the focus back onto Blur and British bands.

Only For Tomorrow, well placed as the opening track, properly saves the album from second tier status. And it is because of the inclusion of this track, which may not have made the album at all were it not for Dave Balfe, that things finally began to change for Blur. Despite the fact it had stalled at number 28 in the charts, it was in a subsequent acoustic performance in the very West London featured in the song, at an outdoor concert to mark the launch of the indie radio station XFM (soon to be huge champions of Britpop and all indie-guitar music) on 13th June 1993, that something finally clicked into place. "The penny dropped," EMI music publisher and friend of the band Mike Smith told John Harris. "From that moment everything went right [for Blur]."

At the end of August that same year Blur headlined the second stage at Reading Festival and, "Suddenly it clicked. The performance clicked," says Graham Coxon in the 2009 documentary *No Distance Left to Run*. "And I remember in the hotel afterwards sitting in this chair," adds Albarn, "and there was the editor of the NME and the editor of the Melody Maker and… I was sitting on this chair, and I was going, 'That was a good day's work.'"[viii]

"That show was probably the most important gig we've ever played," says Alex James in his autobiography. "Chris Morrison gave us all a wedge of cash afterwards and told us not to worry any more."[ix]

Single 6:

Chemical World
Released: 28th June 1993; UK Chart Position: 28; Label: Food; Album: *Modern Life is Rubbish*
B-sides: CD1 (live at Glastonbury 1992): Chemical World (reworked); Never Clever (live); Pressure on Julian (live); Come Together (live)
CD2: Young & Lovely; Es Schmecht; My Ark
7": Maggie May (Rod Stewart & Martin Quittenton)
Producer/s: Stephen Street, Steve Lovell (Maggie May), John Smith (My Ark), Clive Langer and Alan Winstantley (Chemical World reworked)

But the year was far from over for Blur. Two weeks after the XFM gig, Chemical World was released as a single. Frustratingly, yet again, it failed to dent the top 20, despite the growing buzz around them and around Britpop. The band were also set to release Sunday Sunday in October too, finishing out the *Modern Life* campaign, and that too would fail to reach further than the top 30. It was still a long wait until the band garnered any real success in the charts.

The Chemical World single marked the first time the band put out two versions of a CD release. Prompted by two different versions of the lead song, and wishing to find a home for the plethora of material that they had on file after the ill-fated early recordings of their second album, the band decided to also release a live at Glastonbury version of the single.

This tactic was continued with nearly every one of their subsequent single releases, allowing die-hard fans the opportunity of buying both singles, and so pushing the release further up the charts. As fate would have it, this could be viewed as one of the reasons that Country House managed to beat Roll With It to the top spot in August 1995, kill-joys claiming this tactic meant Blur cheated their way to the top.

UK Official Singles Chart – Top 10 – 11th July 1993:

1. Pray – Take That
2. Dreams – Gabrielle
3. What is Love – Haddaway
4. Tease Me – Chake Demus and Pliers
5. What's Up – 4 Non Blondies
6. One Night in Heaven – M People
7. I Will Survive (1993) – Gloria Gaynor
8. (I Can't Help) Falling in Love With You – UB40
9. Will You Be There – Michael Jackson
10. Have I Told You Lately – Rod Stewart

....

28. Chemical World – Blur

Chart music can be a strange beast. Weeks can roll by without a memorable hit, only for three to then come along at once. Some songs manage to gain lasting notoriety despite the number they chart at, and the week that Chemical World stalled at number 28, there was not one but three classic nineties songs, still on repeat at the nineties clubs today, in the top 10. Pray was the first of 12 number 1 singles for Take That, Dreams was a classic in waiting for Gabrielle, and What's Up, although a one hit wonder for 4 Non Blondes, started a career that would lead all the way to the Songwriters Hall of Fame for its writer Linda Perry.

That said, there is a still an inconsistency to the charts at this time. Any chart that features rereleases of hits from past decades: Gloria Gaynor's I Will Survive; or covers of hits from past decades: Elvis' (I Can't Help) Falling in Love With You, and Van Morrison's Have I Told You Lately, isn't exactly looking forwards.

Documentary no. 1

Starshaped
Released: 12th September 1993
Director: Matthew Longfellow

Every band needs a tourumentary made about them, but in one of the key scenes from 1993's *Starshaped*, it looks very much like Blur would immediately come to regret signing up for the film. The four of them sit around a plastic-moulded table, which is undoubtably in a service station somewhere off a motorway in the UK. They are very hung over, which is one of the two states that we see the band in throughout this hour long run through of a year of their touring schedule.

"What they want to know is, what was it like to be in Blur last year [1992]?" asks Damon.

Silence. No-one speaks. Worlds are created and destroyed in the length of the pause, yet still none of the band answer.

"And as you can see, no-one has anything to say about that," adds Damon.

How different that scene would have been back in 1991.

Back when it was released in September 1993, *Starshaped* must have been a difficult watch for those around Blur. Although Longfellow chooses to book end the film with the band members wandering down a grass verge toward, and then away, from the camera, he chooses to frame them next to what looks like an A-road (they're probably just around the corner from that motorway service station), meaning that what was intended as a simple, boyish movement, feels strangely out of place and very uncomfortable.

Rather, it is much better to watch the film from the safety of knowing that it all turns out ok for the group in the end. They experience incredible success with their next album, and although they have their problems over the next decade and a half, they end up friends again at the end of it all. The reason being, that they come across as very likeable people, in a very unlikeable band. Music-wise, there is very little place for anything involving much of a tune here, the pop-stylings of There's No Other Way, for example, and even Bang, would have been a welcome relief from the difficult post-punk of tracks like Day After Day. It is what it must have been like going to see Seymour back in the early days, but with much more at stake.

Although we don't actually see them drinking much, the band seem to be drunk in nearly every scene. One of their perennial problems around this time. Without any of the other stuff, famously linked to the music industry, that helps to sober you up. Graham is lost at an unnamed festival, off on a drunken amble somewhere;

Alex, sent off to find him, quickly loses interest in the search, and ends up partying with some random hangers on; and the camera lingers uncomfortably long on Damon, apparently only too happy to vomit all over his shoes on camera, either having just come off stage, or – please not – head out to perform, again, backstage at some unnamed music festival somewhere.

The film follows the band from their appearance at Reading Festival in August 1991, by way of Glastonbury 1992 (the set of which made it onto the Chemical World CD1 release), but for the most of the film they could be anywhere in the world that has a field, a stage and several thousand drunk revellers in it. Which given what we know about the band around this time, was exactly what they were doing.

The band, but Alex James predominantly, seem to have much posher accents than they do in later years. Either they dumbed down how they spoke amidst an industry that fostered inverse snobbery, or Alex was worn down by the years of industry fatigue.

In later years the film has achieved cult status, particularly in light of the band's latter day success, and was clearly an influence on the hand-held, heavy-cut edited work of Grant Gee and his 1998 Radiohead documentary *Meeting People is Easy*, or Baillie Walsh's 2007 Oasis tourumentary *Lord Don't Slow Me Down*. At the time though, it must have been something of a difficult watch. The claustrophobia of endless Tokyo hotel corridors, or faceless backstage spaces and underground carparks of football stadiums and every-city American arenas, of Gee and Walsh's films, swapped for the permanence of fields and mud and drunk music fans. This is a band who are not at a high level. There is no distance between them and their audience, and it shows. Despite having had what could be called a hit single and a semi-hit album, they are not rock stars, they are still, your mates who are in a band.

"Dangerous hints of melody," says John Peel backstage at Reading. "Must expunge that and you'll go far…" He must be talking about a different band, because there is very little melody involved in Blur's performance throughout *Starshaped.*

Single 7:

Sunday Sunday
Released: 4th October 1993; UK Chart Position: 26; Label: Food; Album: *Modern Life is Rubbish*
B-sides: CD1 (Blur featuring Seymour): Dizzy; Fried; Mixed Up
CD2 (The Popular Community Song CD): Daisy Bell (Harry Dacre); Let's All Go Down the Strand (Murphy, Castling)
7": Tell Me, Tell Me
12": Long Legged; Mixed Up
Producer/s: Steve Lovell, Graeme Holdaway

By far their most complex release to date, the last single of 1993 was positioned as a kind of house clearance with a total of eight additional tracks alongside the A-side, across the three different formats and two CD versions. Like their previous single, the majority of the tracks were included as a way for the band to get rid of their unreleased material, in this instance, the early demoes they had recorded with the Beat Factory, when they were still Seymour. The two other tracks that make up The Popular Community Song CD took the band's direction even further back, to the musical halls of Victorian London: Daisy Bell, better known as A Bicycle Built for Two, was written for one of the future Edward VII's (then the Prince of Wales) many mistresses; and the 1909 song Let's All Go Down the Strand, itself an ode to the theatre district of the London street.

Wearing their influences on their sleeves, Blur were using the nostalgia-soaked subject matter of Sunday Sunday, itself an ode to the simple joys of life on the seventh day, and mixing them with the music hall influences of the time when Britain was the most powerful nation on the planet. It shows how many ideas were floating around the band at the time, and the direction that their thinking was heading.

UK Official Singles Chart – Top 10 – 10th October 1993:

1. Relight My Fire – Take That ft. Lulu
2. I'd Do Anything for Love (But I Won't Do That) – Meatloaf
3. Boom! Shake the Room – DJ Jazzy Jeff and the Fresh Prince
4. Shed Don't Let Nobody – Chaka Demus and Pliers
5. Moving on Up – M People
6. Life – Haddaway
7. Stay – Eternal
8. Relax (1993) – Frankie Goes to Hollywood
9. Hallowed by thy Name – Iron Maiden
10. Go West – Pet Shop Boys

……………………………………

26. Sunday Sunday – Blur

Clearly on the same three-month release schedule as Blur, the top 10 in October 1993 was filled with many of the same artists as their last single, including Take That and their second number 1, Chaka Demus and Pliers, M People and Haddaway. Considering how different each of their acts is, and as such not deemed competition for one another, we can see how in tune with one another the major labels were, and how carefully plotted the release schedules were for all of the artists, no matter what level they were at.

As 1993 marched on, so did the Blur machine continue on its endless tour. After the success of Reading Festival back on the August bank holiday they were back touring lowly UK universities, as term began, and then on to France, Belgium, Sweden, Denmark, Italy, and on to Japan and then America where they played the Whisky a Go Go at the end of November, finishing up the year on 7th December 1993 at the Paradise Rock Club in Boston.

Despite how positive that post-show party at Reading Festival may have seemed, the 30 international dates that they played before the end of the year must have felt like something of a slog. Was it ever going to change? Yes, was the simple answer. By the time of their next gig at the Rock and Solex Festival in France in mid-April 1994, the world to Blur would look like a very different place indeed.

CHAPTER FOUR
Parklife – Success at Last! (1994)

The first new music of 1994, the year that made Blur, came in the form of the pop-tastic stylings of Girls & Boys. Somehow, what they had been saying for the last two years finally made sense and the single chimed with the public like none of their others quite had up to this point. It went straight in at number 5, their highest positioning yet, in March 1994, just in time for summer.

Single 8:

Girls & Boys
Released: 7th March 1994; UK Chart Position: 5; Label: Food; Album: *Parklife*
B-sides: CD1: Magpie; Anniversary Waltz
CD2: People in Europe; Peter Panic
Producer: Stephen Street

With Girls & Boys (and later on, *Parklife*), Blur finally left Seymour behind and created an identity that for better or worse, would stay with them forever. Dave Rowntree's disco beat accompanied by Alex James' most prominent funk bass line to date, support Damon's purposefully simplistic – almost irritating – repeated keyboard chime. Only Graham's guitar, itself a pork pie hat away from *too* jaunty, reminded the listener that this was an indie-rock band, playing at euro-pop, because the repetitive, looped, earworm of a chorus ("girls who want boys, who like boys to be girls, who do boys like they're girls, who do girls like they're boys") was specifically designed to fit the exact surroundings of the Club 18-30 holiday it was aping.

The song was revolutionary. Part piss-take, and part perfect pop-song. Initially the band's existing fans didn't know whether they were allowed to like it or not, particularly when the song gathered momentum on the pre-summer radio playlists, notably on the youth orientated Radio 1, and a plethora of youngsters began turning up to the band's gigs. Today it is a firm fan favourite and has been used to open the band's live sets since they reformed back in 2009.

With the song, Damon used the legendary image of the Club 18-30 holiday, to make a social comment about sex and the modern youth of the UK ("love in the nineties, it's paranoid"). Founded in 1968 to promote cheap Mediterranean holidays for mass groups, Club 18-30 soon carved out a reputation for sending teams of teenagers (19 was the average age) to Corfu, Crete, Ayia Napa, and of course Ibiza, for two weeks of hedonistic partying. As the price of air fares began to fall throughout the seventies, Club 18-30 changed hands (eventually ending up with Thomas Cook in 1998), steadily growing in popularity, until being briefly rebranded as The Club in the early nineties. It finally relaunched itself under its original name in 1994, just as Girls & Boys was coming to prominence. The club found its biggest success over this period.

Then in 1995 came the infamous Saatchi & Saatchi advertising campaign, which received its own backlash due to the perceived promotion of casual sex, but which in turn simply gave the company more publicity. As the Manchester Evening News had it on 20th January 1995, one billboard ad was of "a picture of a male torso wearing underpants mysteriously containing, apparently a grapefruit, [which] says: 'Girls, can we interest you in a package holiday?' In a corner it says, 'Pack your trunks.' Three women artists based in Manchester today described the ads as juvenile, offensive to women and irresponsible. To one poster containing the message: 'You can be drunk and disorderly for two weeks' they have added the words: 'Aids is a life sentence.'"[x]

The relaxing of morals around casual sex, and the ease of access and attitudes toward drug use, notably ecstasy and cocaine, and alcohol, promoted partying, and split the left and right like any key debate. The horrors of the HIV/AIDS crisis of the eighties was still fresh and prominent (AIDS most famous victim Freddie Mercury died in 1991), but the promotion of safe sex in schools meant that by 1994 the attitude was beginning to shift toward freedom of choice, as the generation that had grown up being shown by their teachers how to put a condom onto a banana, were coming of age and ready to try it out…not on a banana.

Similarly, education around drugs and their effects meant that they were no longer simply vilified, and for good or bad, youngsters were given the opportunity of making up their minds about whether to take them or not. The alternative being the tragic case of Leah Betts, who took ecstasy on her eighteenth birthday in November 1995. After experiencing a panic attack her friends forced her to drink 7 litres of water in a 90 minute period, having heard this was the way to help her, and she drowned.

The left and the right blamed each other for her death, the first high-profile loss of life caused in conjunction with ecstasy. Betts' story caught the public attention chiefly because she was from a very typical middle-class background, her father was even a policeman, and it became clear that drugs were ubiquitous within society, and not relegated to the realms of the destitute working-classes, and the characters of *Trainspotting*, and as such, needed to be dealt with by educating the young.

By placing their finger on this twitching nerve of a subject, Blur drew the attention of the public, soon becoming a key catalyst for the changing times. There was nothing vague about the song's message. It went for the jugular, both musically and lyrically placing itself in the forefront of the speakers and a key public conversation, and it paid off, going straight in at number 5 in March 1994, paving the way for the album that was to follow two months later. This was the first example of Blur drawing their subject matter from the immediate world around them and despite its overly jaunty sound, there is a darker side to its message, despite the obvious highs, casual sex and a hedonistic lifestyle can lead to unwanted pregnancy, venereal disease, depression and addiction.

This dual edged message would underpin all of Blur's upcoming work on their first masterpiece, *Parklife.*

UK Official Singles Chart – Top 10 – 13th March 1994:

1. Doop – Doop
2. Without You – Mariah Carey
3. The Sign – Ace of Base
4. Streets of Philadelphia – Bruce Springsteen
5. **Girls & Boys – Blur**
6. Renaissance – M People
7. Pretty Good Year – Tory Amos
8. Return to Innocence – Enigma
9. Like to Move it – Reel 2 Reel ft. Mad Stuntman
10. Breathe Again – Toni Braxton

Doop, by the band Doop (the album was also called *Doop*…well, *Doop Mania*), perhaps the last of the nineties novelty records (unless you count Mike Flowers Pops' version of Wonderwall in 1995), was at number 1 the week that Blur reached number 5, and the remainder of the top 10 is completed by the likes of Ace of Base and Mariah Carey, safe inoffensive pop music that wasn't going to harm anyone. To the untrained eye, Girls & Boys may have looked like it fit into that week's chart as a slice of euro-pop, and perhaps that is where part of its success came from, girls and boys happily chirping along to the catchy chorus with no idea what the song was about. With the release of the album a few weeks later, that would all change.

'It's got nothing to do with Vorsprung durch technique, you know'

<u>Album 3:</u>
Parklife Released: 25th April 1994; UK Chart Position: 1; Label: Food Track Listing: Girls & Boys; Tracy Jacks; End of the Century; Parklife; Bank Holiday; Badhead; The Debt Collector; Far Out; To the End; London Loves; Trouble in the Message Centre; Clover Over Dovoer; Magic America; Jubilee; This is a Low; Lot 105 Producer: Stephen Street

Parklife is not only one of the most important albums of 1994, but of all British music, of all time. It was the first indie-rock album of the nineties to sell a million copies (closely followed by *Definitely Maybe*, released three months later) and started something which British music has not looked back from. Although The Stone Roses' first album had been released in 1989, it was the biggest selling guitar album of the nineties so far, shifting some 300,000 copies and going platinum, creating legends in the process. *Parklife* shifted 27,000 copies on its first week of release, but by Christmas 1994 it was selling 40,000 copies a week, a slow burner that soon led to its total sales of 1.25 million in the UK alone, going four times platinum.[xi] Around the world it sold 2.5million. In comparison, The Smiths' most successful album *The Queen is Dead* went once platinum, meaning it sold 300,000 copies in the UK.

In the UK, *Parklife* has spent 119 weeks on the UK Official Albums Chart, the first run lasting until February 1996, and it appeared again at number 24 in April 2014, celebrating its twentieth anniversary. Symbolically, it knocked another great British rock institution Pink Floyd from the top spot, with their return to form album, *The Division Bell.* The old being forced to make way for the new.

UK Official Albums Chart – Top 10 – 1st May 1994:

1. ***Parklife* – Blur**
2. *The Division Bell* – Pink Floyd
3. *Our Town – Greatest Hits* – Deacon Blue
4. *Stacked Up* – Senser
5. *The Very Best of* – Marvin Gaye
6. *Toni Braxton* – Toni Braxton
7. *A Carnival of Hits* – Judith Durham/Seekers
8. *Happy Nation* – Ace of Base
9. *Everybody Else is Doing It So Why Can't We?* – Cranberries
10. *Music Box* – Mariah Carey

Parklife was the band's most confident album partly, because at two albums in, and nearly four years as professional recording artists, they were well established enough both in a studio and playing live together to know what they were doing. Now that it felt the tide had finally turned in their favour, quality new material flowed out of Damon at such a rate, that the recording of the album came together incredibly quickly. They were putting down demoes before the promotional work for *Modern Life* was even finished, eager to start recording the album proper as soon as they could.

They added Girls & Boys to their live set in the summer of 1993, soon including Parklife, using the festivals of Europe to gauge each new song's popularity. This meant that by the time they played that triumphant show at Reading Festival, they had spent the last few months honing the new songs to a comfortable position. They went straight into the Maison Rouge studios with Stephen Street in September 1993, and the album was completed by early 1994.

In 1994 Britain was a changing place. Led by the rebirth and regeneration of London, the long years of Thatcherite austerity were far behind, and the capital was finding itself carefully gentrified. It was no accident that Canary Wharf can be seen in the background of the video for Parklife, as Damon's jogger makes his way down the East End high street. One Canada Square was four years old by this point, but when you think of how developed Canary Wharf is as a business district today, it appears in the background of the video as a lone beacon, nodding at the future, and the money that would soon pour into the Docklands.

Parklife positioned Blur at the vanguard of change for the country, and the band soon came to represent the new Britain, the youthful Britain, who were about to vote in the youngest Prime Minister for two hundred years. The old, once again, making way for the new. Suede may have had the first number 1 album back in 1993, but *Parklife* made Blur the first phenomenon. When they were joined first by Oasis, and then by Pulp, it became a movement, the most successful since The Beatles and the Stones in the sixties, and this meant the politicians wanted some of it too.

Things Can Only Get Better

Tony Blair inherited the leadership of the Labour party in 1994 by a stroke of chance and near perfect timing, but unfortunately at the cost of a man's life. After his shock defeat at the 1992 general election, the old socialist Neil

Kinnock was succeeded by (the quite literal everyman) John Smith. Much like his counter-part in the Tory held government, Prime Minister John Major, Smith was a safe pair of hands, but a leader who was also looking to modernise the Labour party – he famously did away with the 'en bloc' voting system in favour of the more democratic 'one member one vote' – but not to the same extent that some of the (mostly) younger members of the party were demanding.

One of these members was Blair, a self-proclaimed moderniser, who drew together the weight of the Labour party through his famous 'deal' with the soon to be Chancellor of the Exchequer and his eventual successor, Gordon Brown. Blair and Brown's desires to revolutionise the Labour party may have come to nothing had Smith not tragically and very suddenly died of a heart attack at the age of just 55, on 12th May 1994, one week after Blur had released *Parklife*.

By July (four weeks before Oasis released Live Forever), Blair was Leader of the Opposition and he quickly set to electioneering and setting his plan for modernising the Labour party into action. Blair and Brown began by aligning the party's values with the American Democratic party, and much less in line with the old socialist principles that it was founded on. Before even coming to power he altered Clause IV of the party's constitution, stripping out the party's socialist principles such as "the common ownership of the means of production" (he would not re-nationalise the railways), in favour of offering everyone the opportunity at the same start in life, adding, "The Labour Party is a democratic socialist party. It believes that by the strength of our common endeavour we achieve more than we achieve alone."

Blair drew together the weight of the people along with the support of the wealthy, by promising not to over tax the super-rich as his Labour predecessors had. As history will tell us, the move was a gamble but a well calculated one that made the most of the changing public mood. In many minds, socialism was just another word for communism, and Britain had made their position throughout the Cold War very clear. Thatcher may have made millions jobless in the eighties after closing the coal mines and accepting that three million people would have to sign on, but Blair monopolised on the booming country that she had created and which John Major had steered through a recession. He was able to pick and choose the various aspects of right and left wing principles and put it all under the banner of New Labour. And it worked.

Damon Albarn was the first of the young artists to open talks with the future Prime Minister and his chief spin doctor Alastair Campbell when they were in opposition in 1995, and he went to visit them at the Palace of Westminster in an attempt to see what a new Labour government might be able to do for the youth of the UK. And he was also the first to distance himself two years later, just before New Labour came to power, writing in an article in Face Magazine that "Blair has a worryingly conservative streak" and was no different from the long line of other politicians that had promised so much and delivered so little.

Parklife

The album is kicked into life by the brash in-your-face-ness of Girls & Boys, a festival of debauchery, but setting out their intentions for the album beyond the obvious, the track is quickly juxtaposed by the life of another civil servant gone awry, the oddly named, Tracy Jacks. The song that Colin Zeal wanted to be. Tracy and Colin could indeed work in the same office, but rather than tell the simple story of a businessman obsessed with time, the former's life is as ridiculous as it is mundane.

There is something Reginald Perrin about Jacks' descent into madness. *The Rise and Fall of Reginal Perrin* was a late seventies sitcom starring Leonard Rossiter as the eponymous oppressed middle-manager driven to erratic and often insane behaviour by the mundanity of his existence. Perrin's story is as absurd as a Kafka novel, yet remains resolutely British. Which other nation would accept such a dull existence with a stiff upper lip? After having faked his suicide twice already, the third series ended with Perrin contemplating it again, before disappearing for good. It is left up to the audience to decide what happened to him. He is notably absent from the fourth season (mostly because Rossiter had died in 1984), bought back by the BBC, 17 years after the third series, in September 1996. *The Legacy of Reginald Perrin* finds the key characters that Perrin left behind only able to inherit from his will if they do something truly absurd. We never find out if Perrin is really dead, once again, it is left up to the audience to decide. It is very likely that the reboot came about due to the focus on such stories by Blur.

In the Blur song, the catalyst for Jacks' downfall is his visit to the Harley Street Doctor "Who prescribed healthy living". He isn't ill, he just needs to look after himself. But this isn't what Jacks wants to hear, "I'd love to stay here and be normal, but it's just so overrated," he says. So one morning he gets on the train to Walton and – just like Perrin – runs around naked on the beach. But he doesn't kill himself by walking into the sea, rather he can't go through with it, and instead is arrested and escorted home. Then he bulldozes his house down on a Tuesday morning. The ending to his story left as open to interpretation as that of Perrin's. It is the subtlety of Tracy Jacks' story that makes it so captivating. In exactly the same way that the obviousness of Stereotypes a year later, makes it the opposite.

Parklife, it therefore seems, is not going to be a light album. In fact, despite the overall feeling of jauntiness that pervades throughout, these are tales of sadness, loneliness and disappear, all wrapped up in a package of hum-able tunes and singles that would be superglued to the radio for the next five years. The poet TS Elliot said that "Immature poets imitate; mature poets steal" and on *Parklife*, Blur lift their influences from a wide variety of places, melding them together and transferring them to the page, making the album greater than the sum of its parts.

In juxtaposing the mostly jolly tunes with grave lyrical content, Damon is calling on his drama training, using the work of the German theatre practitioner Bertolt Brecht, whose chief teaching was to alienate the audience so they did not become lost in the story, but rather focused on the meaning behind the story. Why else call such a genial instrumental tune The Debt Collector, a figure who personifies the bleak connotations of class and poverty. Rather, you might expect a tune called The Debt Collector to sound dark or foreboding, not led by Graham Coxon's cheerful baritone saxophone.

Lyrically, Damon's chief influence on the album is the 1989 novel by Martin Amis, *London Fields*, which he read when the band were touring America. Despite its Hackney district name, the novel is set in Notting Hill, where Damon was living with girlfriend Justine Frischmann. The novel is ostensibly a murder mystery, Nicola Six, aware that she will be killed, goes looking for her killer, but the book is really about the cast of bizarre, colourful characters living life on its own terms, just the wrong side of legal. This is Martin Amis' chief strength as a writer, his books aren't about *what* happens, but what is happening all around. The characters that live in the world of the book, and the bizarre everyday rituals of their existence.

The novel is filled with these characters, whose craziness is, on the page, presented as decidedly normal, even mundane. Characters like the wily Keith Talent, a favourite of Amis, who is described in the very first line as: "…a very bad guy. You might even say that he was the worst guy."[xii] Keith isn't really a bad guy, for one thing, he isn't very good at violence, so instead, rather than earn an honest living, he cheats people in whatever ways he can think of.

With Talent in mind, it is easy to see how Damon made the leap to the protagonist of the song Parklife: "I get up when I want, except on Wednesdays when I get rudely awaken by the dustman. I put my trousers on, have a cup of tea, and think about leaving the house." The devil is in the details. It is the individual specificities of the characters, their own distinct foibles, that make them so intriguing.

Nothing much happens to the character in Parklife. He watches life go on around him, gets up, drinks his tea and feeds the pigeons, the whole time taking in the world around him, contented with his own little place within it. Why is he not at work? What does he do to get by? We are never told, and we don't ask, but what we do know, is that he is not Tracy Jacks. His contentedness at the world around him throws the world on its head. Surely Jacks, with his stable job and house should be the contented one, not the one running around naked on the Wilton beach, or bulldozing his house down. What we are told about the draw of a normal life: a job, a house, a family, have all been thrown into disarray, and we're only on the fourth track.

The album continues like this, jumping from story to story as the tracks wind their way through a labyrinth of life lived in strange but fascinating circumstances, finally culminating in the epic anthem, This is a Low. Alex James says that this track was the only one on the album that they struggled with in the studio, finally finding a breakthrough at the eleventh hour (just as they had done with For Tomorrow a year earlier) when Damon wrote the lyrics around the shipping broadcast, drawn from a tea-towel that James had given him for Christmas. It was a suitable way to round out a strange, but wonderful album, after all, what is more British than the shipping forecast? Despite not being released as a single, the song later became the band's most popular, being played live to huge applause on many occasions.

Parklife is the album the critics and fans wanted *Modern Life is Rubbish* to be. Of the sixteen tracks, unlike most Blur albums, there are no fillers, and each successive song adds something to the whole not already explored on the previous track. End of the Century follows the twenty-something youth experience leading toward the twenty-first century; Jubilee, the closest punk-rock track familiar to the band's former life as Seymour, tells the story of a computer game obsessed youth, the modern-day update of the classic teenage spotty nerd; London Loves, Trouble in the Message Centre and Clover Over Dover are each variations on a theme that prod at the British focused story that runs throughout; and the one-two punch of Bank Holiday and Badhead tell a dual story of the newly acquired British tradition (inherited from the USA) of barbeques and beer on the public holidays, and the story of the morning after. Perhaps modern life isn't so rubbish after all. Or if it is, then it certainly isn't boring.

There is, however, another reading to Badhead.

So far, I've not really stayed in touch,
well I knew as much,
it's no surprise that today,
I get up around two,
with a lack of anything to do.

As can sadly so often be the case, just as Damon Albarn was gaining everything he thought he wanted, his mental state was heading sharply downhill. Depression in young men was becoming more and more common in the mid-nineties, and for various reasons it seemed to be more prominent in young popstars. A combination of living too fast, drinking too much, taking too many drugs and not sleeping enough, combined with emersion in a laddish environment that discouraged sensitivity, positioning it as weakness, meant that too many young men were pushing themselves too hard and not seeking the relevant help when they needed it.

Guigsy, the quiet bass player from Oasis, suddenly dropped out of the band after discovering he was suffering from nervous exhaustion around the release of Wonderwall; Alan McGee, the head of Creation Records and the man that discovered Oasis, collapsed from a similar type of nervous exhaustion after two years of living on nothing but barbiturates and cocaine; Richey Edwards from the Manic Street Preachers disappeared on 1st February 1995, after a troubled past that included bouts of anorexia and self-harm; and of course, in America, Kurt Cobain, the chronic heroin addict, shot himself in April 1994, telling the world that it was better to burn out than to fade away.

Damon Albarn's own depression became manifest in his struggle to get out of bed for days on end, despite the band's newfound success. In his case it was also partly to do with the amount of attention that he was receiving, and his need to always be 'on'. He would walk into a room and everyone would turn to stare at him, whether they had something nice to say or something bad, he had to deal with it all.

Despite his own experiences though, sadly Albarn failed to highlight the need to step away from the reductive negative attitude toward the perceived weakness of mental illness, fostered by the culture of the mid-nineties, therefore only fuelling the issue further. It would be another twenty years before any real positive change was seen in this area.

In 2019 the UK grime artist Dave drew direct reference to the need young men have for professional help with mental illness, framing his 2019 Mercury Music Prize winning album, the aptly named *PSYCHODRAMA*, around a visit to his counsellor, complete with quotes from the man himself included on the record. So showing the world that it is not weak to discuss any psychological issues one might be experiencing. In 2020 Irish indie-rock band The Murder Capital claimed that in the sixties we were going through a sexual revolution, now it's an emotional one.

Single 9:

To the End
Released: 30th May 1994; UK Chart Position: 16; Label: Food; Album: *Parklife*
B-sides: CD1: Threadneedle Street; Got Yer!
CD2: Girls & Boys (Pet Shop Boys 7" remix); Girls & Boys (Pet Shop Boys 12" remix)
Producer: Stephen Street

UK Official Singles Chart – Top 10 – 11th June 1994:

1. Love is All Around – Wet Wet Wet
2. Baby I Love Your Way – Big Mountain
3. You Don't Love Me (No, No, No) – Dawn Penn
4. No Good (Start the Dance) – Prodigy
5. Get-A-Way – Maxx
6. Absolutely Fabulous – Absolutely Fabulous
7. Don't Turn Around – Ace of Base
8. Swamp Thing – Grid
9. Anytime You Need a Friend – Mariah Carey
10. Come on your Reds –

Manchester United Football Squad

....

16. To the End – Blur

To the End, one of Damon Albarn's favourite Blur tracks, reached a not excellent, not dispiriting number 16 when released as a single in June 1994. It had only been a month since the album shocked everyone when it went straight in at number 1, and perhaps too soon for a single that everyone already owned on the album, to come out.

The song, now considered to be one the band's finest moments, is slow, careful and considered, its epic chorus, taken from a comic book "you and I collapsed in love", perhaps too ahead of its time in its calls of saying that "we made it to the end". To the end of what? How many other nineties singles were led by a glockenspiel riff though?

All the People

The release of the album was followed by a celebratory tour of the UK, that was woefully out of synch with how big the band had become in a very short space of time, playing such dizzy heights as Nottingham Rock City, the Wolverhampton Civic Hall and the Ipswich Corn Exchange. The capacities of these venues showed the lack of faith Food Records had in the band after *Modern Life* failed to catch fire, and the dates quickly sold out, the venues all full to bursting, which if anything, helped fuel the legend further. As Louise Wener of support band Sleeper explains in *Live Forever* something changed on that tour:

> *[The venue] was jam packed with 15, 16, 17 and 18 year old kids, and this was a generation that had only known one establishment, one order, literally the whole*

> *lot of them had grown up under Thatcherism and beyond, and there was a sense of excitement that something was changing, perhaps, perhaps this music was foreshadowing something else.*

The kids were cottoning on in their droves and the galleries shook with the excited enthusiasm of the assembled masses. As a piece of propaganda, *Parklife* worked hard at reframing the story of Britain in the nineties and Blur found themselves defining the zeitgeist. The music gave confidence to the people – all the people – to change the way they lived. Life imitating art imitating life. This in turn helped forge the wave that Tony Blair was creating, promising to make very real changes to the country that would be felt for decades to come. Pop music was defining the nation, and Blur were leading the charge.

Single 10:

Parklife
Released: 22nd August 1994; UK Chart Position: 10;
Label: Food; Album: *Parklife*
B-sides: CD1: Supa Shoppa; Theme from an Imaginary Film
CD2: Beard; To the End (French Version)
Producer: Stephen Street

UK Official Singles Chart – Top 10 – 28th August 1994:

1. Love is All Around – Wet Wet Wet
2. Compliments on Your Kiss – Red Dragon with Brian and Tony
3. Crazy for You – Let Loose
4. 7 Seconds – Youssou N'Dour ft. Neneh Cherry

5. Searching – China Black
6. I'll Make Love to You – Boyz II Men
7. I Swear – All-4-One
8. What's Up – DJ Miko
9. Regulate – Warren G & Nate Dogg
10. **Parklife – Blur**

Despite it just denting the top 10, Parklife would go on to be Blur's biggest selling single to date, shifting some 190,000 units.[xiii] The album title track grabbed the attention of the listener due in part to its incredibly sing-a-long chorus, but also because of its spoken word verses, provided courtesy of the actor Phil Daniels, famed for his appearance as the dispirited mod Jimmy in the 1978 film by The Who, *Quadrophenia.* Again, Blur found themselves pushing the boundaries of what was and wasn't acceptable in nineties pop music. No other acts would have dreamt of including a spoken word verse in a pop song. But what Albarn does, is draw the focus of the song to the words that Daniels is speaking, rather than on a melody. Again, employing Brechtian techniques that allow the meaning behind the lyric to come to the fore.

The lyric, semi-nonsensical, follows the voyeuristic habit ("habitual voyeur") of those without work, happy to watch the world go by. It is about life in London parks and those associated with it: binmen, park keepers, joggers, pigeons. Today, Parklife is undoubtably one of the defining songs of Britpop, and in the UK, probably the one most directly related to Blur's work and sound (that honour goes to Song 2 in the rest of the world). For better or worse, it would come to define what many people in the UK still think of as Blur. Although Damon later said the song was written with Hyde Park in mind, the music video focuses its attention on the NW6 post code, which encompasses Kilburn and Kensal Rise, North West London.

Released on 22nd August, Parklife found its way into the charts three weeks after Oasis' released another era-defining single, Live Forever. The Manchester band's third single was a marked turning point in their fortunes (it also reached number 10), and paved the way for the year's other million selling album, *Definitely Maybe*, released the Monday after Parklife charted on the Sunday. The table was set for the show down, exactly a year away.

The rest of 1994 was a blur (sorry!) of touring dates, with the band back in America, where Girls & Boys became their most successful single since There's No Other Way, reaching 60 in the Billboard Top 100. They played nine dates across North America, with Pulp supporting in Hollywood, and then were back in the UK at the beginning of October, to tour across Europe, heading to Japan, where they were huge stars, in November. Meaning they were away when their eleventh single, the last from *Parklife*, and last until Country House in August 1995, End of the Century, was released on 7th November.

Single 11:

End of the Century
Released: 7th November 1994; UK Chart Position: 17;
Label: Food; Album: *Parklife*
B-sides: Red Necks (Coxon); Alex's Song (James)
Producer: Stephen Street

UK Official Singles Chart – Top 10 – 13th November 1994:

1. Baby Come Back – Pato Banton
2. Another Night – MC Sar & The Real McCoy
3. Let Me Be Your Fantasy – Baby D

4. Always – Bon Jovi
5. All I Wanna Do – Sheryl Crow
6. Oh Baby I… – Eternal
7. She's Got that Vibe – R Kelly
8. Sight for Sore Eyes – M People
9. True Faith ('94) – New Order
10. Saturday Night – Whigfield

……………………………

19. End of the Century – Blur

Peaking at number 19, one position lower than arch-rival Suede's tender ode to lost love The Wild Ones, End of the Century was Blur's lowest charting single since Sunday Sunday a year ago, and although it reached the top 20, all it did was fuel the fire that *Parklife* was not a singles album, like *The Great Escape* would be, but rather, a concept album that it is difficult to take the singles out of the context of. People didn't buy the single because unlike Oasis, for example, Blur were not a band known for the quality of their B-sides, and because they would rather buy the album. If however the single's job is to help promote the album, then End of the Century did just this, and sales for *Parklife* peaked as Christmas 1994 approached.

Alongside Suede, finally the charts were starting to be infiltrated by indie-rock music, with the rerelease of New Order's anthem True Faith, remixed and reaching the top 10. A year later, the dance-pop of the likes of the Real McCoy would be in the minority, and Britpop would be the dominate genre.

Blur finished off 1994 with Damon hosting *Top of the Pops*, an honour not afforded many pop singers, introducing Oasis' fifth single of the year, Whatever, and beginning what was soon to become a bitter rivalry.

CHAPTER FIVE
The Great Escape – The People's Prick – Falling Fortunes (1995)

Still riding high from the success of 1994 and *Parklife*, Blur's 1995 started as well as the previous one had ended. Inspired by the fact their music was finally connecting with audiences on a large scale, the band headed straight into the studio to record its follow up, breaking the recording with just one live gig, at the 2,300 capacity Kentish Town Forum on 23rd January. Trying out new material live before recording it was Blur's preferred tactic of deciding what would end up on their new album, and after its enthusiastic outing, Stereotypes was picked to be the next single. That was until the band played Country House at their huge homecoming concert at the Mile End racetrack in June.

Before all of that though Blur and *Parklife* found themselves nominated for four awards at that year's Brit Awards, hosted by Chris Evans, the growing face of Britpop on the TV, at the 10,000 capacity Alexandra Palace in North London. The band had sold out the venue the previous October, and they opened the show with a spirited performance of Girls & Boys before winning all four awards they were nominated for.

Brit Awards won:

- British Album of the Year – *Parklife*
- British Single of the Year – Parklife (Girls & Boys was also nominated)
- British Video of the Year – Parklife
- British Band of the Year

To this day it is still the most amount of awards won in a single night by a single artist, nearly equalled the following year by Oasis, who won three, being pipped to the post for single of the year by Take That's Back for Good. "When I woke up in the morning, I knew my life had changed forever," says Alex James on winning four Brits. "We'd won everything going; it was a record-breaking haul. Blur had become a household name over the course of the evening."[xiv]

And it seems that this is where the rivalry between Blur and Oasis took its first major step forward. On winning the best album award, Damon, leading a very drunk rabble of Blur members up to the podium, magnanimously stated that the award should have been shared with Oasis. "Why on earth did I say that?" Damon rhetorically said fifteen years later in *No Distance Left to Run*. What was intended as altruistic came across to the Oasis camp as patronising, and like two opposing football teams, competition between the two camps would soon reach boiling point in the August Battle of Britpop show down.

For the moment though, Blur were contented with their haul and returned to the studio triumphant, to continue recording what would eventually become *The Great Escape*. Everything seemed to be continuing on the way up, Damon had even learned to deal with his depression by channelling it into the songs on the album, separating out his own worries and fears from the band's success. As it would soon emerge, the key themes of the new album would soon transpire to be loneliness and isolation.

With the album in the bag, the band played a tiny secret warmup gig at the Dublin Castle on 18th May. This was a trick they would continue long into the new millennium, and their reformation in 2009, playing to a tiny invited audience in order to prepare themselves for a major gig, in this instance the massive concert at Mile End stadium to 27,000 eager fans on 17th June.

Broadcast live on Radio 1, the Mile End gig was intended as a triumphant homecoming. The stadium was more used to housing sporting events rather than huge rock concerts, but the quintessentially cockney setting on the edge of the City of London square mile fit perfectly with the band's current aesthetic and the concert was deemed a huge success.

The mammoth 23 song set leant heavily on the *Parklife* material, but also included the best bits of *Modern Life*: Sunday Sunday, Chemical World, Advert, For Tomorrow and Popscene. Only She's So High survives from the first album, showcasing how the band had drawn a line under their auspicious start. New songs Stereotypes and Globe Alone were also played, as was the brass led oompah band number they had all thought would be a B-side, until the audience's reaction. The performance cemented it as the band's next single, and Country House was pencilled in for release on 1st August 1995.

Before that though, things began to heat up with Blur's growing rivalry with Oasis, when the Manchester group scored their first number 1 single Some Might Say on 5th May, achieving what no other indie had done for a decade or more.

Alex James was living in Soho at this time, and was making a name for himself as one of the foremost party-boys of the pop scene. His cohorts included the future members of Fat Les: Damien Hirst and Keith Allen, and his nightly haunts included the Groucho Club and the Mars Bar, the latter of which James offered as a venue for Oasis' celebration party for reaching number 1. James booking the venue meant that Blur were invited, and it was at this party that Liam Gallagher goaded the band about their number 1. The fight was on.

Battle of the Bands and the Classes

Perhaps Damon thought it should have been Blur with the first number 1 single, or Liam's crowing had managed to get to him, but Damon's next move drew attention to Britpop for all the wrong reasons. On finding out that Oasis' next single was due for release on 14th August, Damon convinced Food Records to move the release of Country House to the same date. From the Oasis side, label head Alan McGee suggested moving their release date so the two singles would not compete in the charts, but the band refused, and the field was set for the type of showdown that the music industry had been at pains to avoid for thirty years, and which has still not been repeated to this date.

Damon was only too happy to play the game, and on paper it looked like Blur set themselves up for an easy win. Firstly, Country House was to be the first single from their new album, the single released that historically performs best in the charts, whilst Oasis' would be the second single from the album. Blur nearly always released two versions of their singles, meaning that fans could buy both versions, pushing the single further up the charts, safe in the knowledge they were still playing the game. Oasis released only one. The music video for Country House was directed by Alex James' best mate Damien Hirst, the most famous and successful of the YBAs, who was about to win the Turner Prize, thus drilling right into Cool Britannia. Oasis' music video was a simple live performance. It looked and felt like Blur were tied directly into the pulse of the nation, and simply wanted it more.

Once both singles were released, the week long wait for the announcement stretched out ahead of both bands like an ice age. Damon was everywhere, being interviewed on the evening news wishing both bands the best of luck, and then on Wednesday 16th August, hosting *Britpop Now*, a show that staged live performances from

Elastica, Powder, Menswear, Pulp, The Boo Radleys, Supergrass, and of course Blur, but not Oasis. Tellingly, Dave Rowntree fled the country for the South of France to avoid the growing media focus, Alex James relocated to Devon with Damien Hirst, and Graham Coxon withdrew to the safety of Camden. Oasis didn't seem to be around at all, but their presence was felt by the multitude of fans buying their single, and the constant plays on the radio. Damon seemed to carry the whole affair on his shoulders, and he also knew the result before anyone else. At the celebration party on the Sunday night Graham dragged everyone back to earth by attempting to jump out of the window, solidly making his feelings known about how far he felt the whole thing had gone.

Since *Parklife*, Blur had worked hard at creating a cartoon image of a band not unlike The Beatles in *A Hard Day's Night*, or the Monkees TV series. There was a blasé silliness to the band of Parklife and Girls & Boys, that had drawn them millions of teenage followers, and nowhere was this more apparent than on Country House, particularly when the song was compared to the rock 'n' roll seriousness of Oasis' Roll With It.

Damon had constructed the cartoon image of himself, which he would spend the next couple of years doing his best to distance himself from. He understood the concept of pop star as idealised image, an avatar for fans to vicariously live their lives through, even if what fans saw had no real connection to the person the pop star really is. Not entirely blamelessly, fans would not be able to strip away the Damon pop star image, from the real person, something he would discover all too well as 1995 bore on. This is at least partly why Damon would later create an entirely fictional band with Gorillaz, affording him the opportunity of constructing exactly what he wanted them to look and sound like, with no link to himself.

On Sunday 20th August Radio 1 announced that Blur won the battle, giving Blur their first number 1 single.

The real winner of the Battle of Britpop however was the singles market, which by the mid-nineties had been struggling for sales. A win-win for the record companies. Even if Oasis did come second, they still shifted 216,000 copies of a single that would otherwise have sold half of that. Country House sold 274,000 in that first week, making it one of the fastest selling number 1 singles of all time. Surely the future was theirs for the taking.

Single 12:

Country House
Released: 14th August 1995; UK Chart Position: 1;
Label: Food; Album: *The Great Escape*
B-sides: CD1: One born Every Minute; To the End ft. Françoise Hardy
CD2: Girls & Boys; Parklife; For Tomorrow (all recorded live at Mile End Stadium on 17th June 1995)
Producer: Stephen Street

UK Official Singles Chart – Top 10 – 20th August 1995:

1. **Country House – Blur**
2. Roll With It – Oasis
3. I Luv U Baby – Original
4. Never Forget – Take That
5. Waterfalls – TLC
6. Everybody – Clock
7. Son of a Gun – JX
8. Human Nature – Madonna
9. Kiss from a Rose/I'm Alive – Seal
10. Try Me Out – Corona

Despite the whole country turning around and noticing what was going on in the formerly shaded indie music scene, by the end of 1995 the tide had shifted dramatically against Blur in favour of the era-defining Oasis, and with hindsight it becomes clear that this was always the inevitable conclusion. Blur could only lose from the association, whilst Oasis could only succeed. It would have made sense for the underdogs, Oasis, to engage the more successful group in such a battle, in an effort to draw on their bigger profile, but not the other way around. Oasis' first album had been a huge success and their last single Some Might Say had reached number 1, but they were still too early in their career to have their position cemented in place, whereas Blur, three albums in, had only just managed to secure their place after years of hard work. As Alan McGee put it, "Look, if you're a prize fighter and you're on top, don't invite the newcomer into the ring with you, cos' it doesn't matter whether he wins or loses, he's won at the end of it, because you're now at the same level."[xv]

The ultimate result would be that everything Albarn and his band did for the next few years would be judged in comparison to the achievements of Oasis, which would have been fine, had the Manchester band not emerged as one of the most successful British groups since The Beatles.

Oasis' reaction to the Battle of Britpop was to saunter on as if nothing had happened and then release their era-defining second album *(What's the Story) Morning Glory?* in early October, followed in quick succession by their most successful single Wonderwall, and then to headline the biggest indoor concerts in Europe, when they sold out two nights at the 20,000 capacity Earls Court, in early November 1995. The latter belittling Blur's achievements at courting 27,000 thousand fans to Mile End in May.

Blur were missing for most of the rest of 1995, with another pointless tour of an America that was proving it did not care about them. Their absence was easily filled by the overarching and obvious presence of the Gallagher brothers and co., and although he had never fully adjusted to the harsh focus of the spotlight, Damon Albarn liked it even less when it was shifted away from him.

Best Days...Fade Away

Album 4:

The Great Escape
Released: 11th September 1995; UK Chart Position: 1; Label: Food
Track Listing: Stereotypes; Country House; Best Days; Charmless Man; Fade Away; Top Man; The Universal; Mr Robinson's Quango; He Thought of Cars; It Could Be You; Ernold Same; Globe Alone; Dan Abnormal; Entertain Me; Yuko and Hiro
Producer: Stephen Street

UK Official Albums Chart – Top 10 – 17th September 1995:

1. ***The Great Escape* – Blur**
2. *One Hot Minute* – Red Hot Chili Peppers
3. *Stanley Road* – Paul Weller
4. *Crazysexycool* – TLC
5. *Circus* – Lenny Kravitz
6. *HIStory – Past Present and Future Book 1* – Michael Jackson
7. *Zeitgeist* – The Levellers
8. *The Charlatans* – The Charlatans
9. *Dummy* – Portishead
10. *Definitely Maybe* – Oasis

With *Parklife* still very much alive at number 16 (*Modern Life* at 33, and *Leisure* at 45) the week that *The Great Escape* went straight in at number 1, the albums chart of September 1995 was shaping up into a veritable who's who of classic music still talked about 25 years later, with Blur in poll position. British and Irish indie-rock bands like Supergrass, the Cranberries, Black Grape, and Radiohead were filling the albums charts with incredibly popular long players, as were American rock bands such as the Foo Fighters and Offspring. Hip-hop dance acts in the form of Massive Attack, Leftfield, M People were treading new ground for sampled music, and quality pop music from Take That, Seal, Celine Dion, and Sheryl Crow was flooding the air waves.

It was quite simply an incredible time for music, and *The Great Escape* should have been the crowning moment of glory for Britpop kings Blur. The album shifted 350,000 copies in its first week alone, going immediately platinum, and going on to sell 1.05 million in the UK, 122,000 in the USA and 2.54 million worldwide, making it their most successful album to date.[xvi] The critical response was also quite incredible, with the NME giving it 9 out of 10, and Melody Maker famously awarding it 12 out of 10. The stage was set for Blur to slip seamlessly from the country's biggest band into the world's, taking their stories of contemporary British life out on the road, at the exact moment that Britain was rechristening itself as Cool Britannia. So what on earth went wrong?

The Great Escape

As previously discussed, *The Great Escape* is another album that Blur attempted to root in its modern Britishness. But what exactly did that look like on this third attempt at doing so? And how had this tactic developed since *Modern Life* and *Parklife*?

Firstly, Damon positions himself as one of Britain's greatest young song writers. On Mr Robinson's Quango, for example, he takes the idea of the titular government initiative of awarding power to local organisations, in order to tell the story of a sleazy middle-manager. Not that Damon could have known it in 1995, but quangos would later form a solid part of Tony Blair's funding strategy between 1997 and 2010, only to be abolished for wasting money, under the David Cameron led Tory/Lib Dem coalition government. The most famous example being the UK Film Council, which was dissolved in 2011, its powers for film funding given back to the British Film Institute in April 2011.

Therefore, either by chance or intuition born from experience, Damon proved to showcase a gift for rooting a song in a very contemporary moment, that years later would stand as a historical document for that moment in time. Alongside Lennon and McCartney, and Paul Weller, one of the other great songwriters to do this was Damon's hero, Ray Davies, who employed the same trick on The Kinks' classics Dedicated Follower of Fashion, Dead End Street and Sunny Afternoon.

Damon was therefore slipping seamlessly into the ranks of the greatest of Britain's songwriters, however, where *Modern Life* paved the way, working hard to set the scene by offering the broad strokes of traits of contemporary life on tracks like Advert (consumerism was rife across the whole world, not just the UK), and *Parklife* effortlessly drew an accurate picture of life in contemporary Britain through a wry wit and furtive wink to the camera, *The Great Escape* felt like it was trying too hard to be a Blur album. The last of the Britpop or 'life' trilogy (the band tried hard to fit the word 'life' into the title, but eventually gave up), was filled with listenable tunes, but it quickly became clear that as an album it was simply treading the same water, produced from the comfortable position of success. Therefore, lacking any real edge. Ironically, this meant that the writers of the album itself became like characters from a Blur song. Fitting really.

The album's cover paints a vivid picture. Moving away from the classic historical achievement of the past – with the Mallard Pullman train on *Modern Life*, and the salt-of-the-earth Britishness of the whippets on *Parklife* – it in part parodies David Hockney's 1967 painting *A Bigger Splash*. A reference yet again to the artistic achievements of the sixties, and also to the opulence of success.

The title, also an intertextual reference to the classic 1963 film, about a largely failed attempt to escape a German prisoner of war camp during the Second World War (the film really should have been called The Terrible Escape), could be read in a number of ways. Just what are the band trying to escape from? Their success? Themselves? The normal life, that pop stardom is an escape from? But when the title sits alongside the album cover, another picture is painted entirely. The female feet in the foreground show someone diving into the sea without a care in the world, but the position of the two men in the boat behind gives the image a much more sinister tone. Is she escaping from them?

This ambiguity carries itself into the songs and to the awkward feeling of dislocation and discomfort that permeates the album. A feeling replicated in the press' views. It is rare that records receive such strong reviews, and even rarer for the same critics to turn around and disown their initial opinions just weeks later. Q Magazine, riding high on Blur proving themselves triumphant after the Battle of Britpop, would later issue an apology for their five-star review.[xvii] Whereas the exact opposite would be the case for Oasis' soon to be released second album, *(What's the Story) Morning Glory?*, which after having lacklustre reviews, on its release on 2nd October 1995, went on to enrapture its audience.

The critics peculiar about turn could be put down to cynical magazine editors realising that they could sell more copies by aping the opinions of the populous, who had now decided Oasis were the better band, but still, even today, there persists the feeling that the album is schizophrenic in nature, perhaps more so than any in modern British musical history. As Stuart McMahon says in his BBC review of the album in 2011, the album is "polarizing, messy, yes. But soulful and quite wonderful, too."[xviii]

Unlike the other two albums in the 'life' trilogy, *The Great Escape* probably isn't more than the sum of its parts. Just like its predecessors, the songs on the album are inconsistent in their quality, yet again, the band insisted on including fifteen tracks when eleven would have done, and the likes of the terribly titled He Thought of Cars and the overly quirky It Could be You (to all intents and purposes the same song), would not have been missed if left off. That said, the production is sleeker than on any of their previous work, Stephen Street once again able to mine directly into the band's consciousness and deliver their demands directly onto disc, and the band are playing at the top of their game; but there is an unnecessary busyness to most of the songs, with string and brass sections included to fill out the sound, meaning that the listener is left with the feeling that something is missing, and ultimately drawing focus to the lack of substance to much of the material.

Things begin on solid enough ground with Stereotypes, the album's third single, and its cheeky catch phrase, later splashed across the front of the single cover: "Wife swapping is your future!". The song picks up quite nicely from where Girls & Boys left off. The subjects of *Parklife*'s lead single now grown up and looking to spice up their dwindling sex lives. The song provides a promising start to the album, but as a statement of intent its obviousness is its major strength as well as its downfall, just like the album that it represents. Listeners have heard this before, just a year ago when Girls & Boys was released. Where is the new direction, does the audience need *Parklife* part II?

Stereotypes gives way to Country House and it becomes clear that this album is set to be loud and bombastic, with the brass parts that the band toyed with on *Parklife* – remember Graham Coxon's plodding pomp-pomp on Parklife – now in full brass band flow. The final refrain, played by the Britpop-go-to brass band outfit The Kick Horns, is so perfectly composed by Damon Albarn, that once heard it feels as if you've heard it many times before, on a track by Queen perhaps, or ELO, or most clearly on Penny Lane era Beatles. As Martin Power puts it, "'Country House' brought together all that was good, bad and totally absurd about Blur in one huge burst of primary colours."[xix] It's subject matter, it's huge sound and the whole chart battle thing, meant that it cast an unavoidable shadow over the rest of the album.

Track 3 Best Days is something of an overlooked gem for the album. Its subtle, sombre melody and lyric juxtaposing its cheery seeming title. The song is anything but cheery: "Other people would turn around and laugh at you, if you said that these were the best days of our lives." Not 'your', 'our'. On first glance the song appears to be a simple ode to the miserable nature of commuter existence: "Bow bells say goodbye to the last train, over the river they all go again, out into the leafy nowhere, hope someone waiting out there for them." But just like another Ray Davies classic Waterloo Sunset, the song is told from the point of view of the voyeur, perhaps Albarn himself, watching the trains, silently hoping that the inhabitants are happy, deflecting his own melancholia. It's something of a gem for Albarn's song writing, but after the pomp and vigour of Country House, it is over before the audience even know it has started, quickly giving way to the album's final single Charmless Man, which Stuart McMahon described as "so fundamentally rubbish it could snugly sit on the second side of *Leisure*."[xx]

The brass are back on Fade Away, a song, completed with another of Damon's jaunty piano breaks, that is so musically middle of the road, that the story of familiarity breeding contempt, loses the power it could have had were the lyrics used on *Parklife*. Like a poem by Philip Larkin, the couple "stumbled into their lives, in a vague way became man and wife…All they want to do is fade away." It seems that as Damon's lyrics become stronger the complacency of the band's music has driven them into a safe space notoriously dangerous in rock 'n' roll. The music is fine, the melodies rise and fall, the guitars chime away and the rhythm section ambles along in the background, but this was once the band that played such frantic live sets, they often didn't make it to the end. What would that band have thought of a track like Top Man, or the drudgery of Ernold Same?

Single 13:

The Universal
Released: 13th November 1995; UK Chart Position: 5; Label: Food; Album: *The Great Escape*
B-sides: CD1: Ultranol; No Monsters in Me; Entertain Me (The Live It! remix)
CD2: Mr Robinson's Quango; It Could Be You; Stereotypes (all live at the BBC)
Producer: Stephen Street

The album's centre point and strongest track was also its second single, The Universal. A song that today has managed to claim status as one of the band's and the audience's favourites. It has closed their live sets since their reformation in 2009.

With a sterling string riff, every bit as withheld and restrained as Country House's brass refrain is over the top and grandiose, the song is completed with simple guitar jabs from Coxon and an epic chorus that pushes the track into the top echelons of the band's work. Again though, when it was released, it was so starkly different to Country House that its message about fears of modern technology distancing people (yet another prophetic nod by Albarn, to the advent and dominance of social media) fell slightly flat, and it reached number 5, when it should have been number 1.

Perhaps the song was too subtle at a time when the band's reputation was for the exact opposite, but the band didn't help themselves by releasing the song with a video based on the 1971 Stanley Kubrick film *A Clockwork Orange*. The video was directed by the modern day genius Jonathan Glazer, known today for directing *Sexy Beast* (2000) and *Under the Skin* (2013), but who made his name through directing music videos for the likes of Radiohead (Street Spirit) and Jamiroquai (Virtual Insanity).

The video for The Universal was one of the band's finest, and today it is considered a classic, however, it missed the mark at the time because no-one had seen the source material. Back in 1973, on fearing the film too controversial due to its depiction of sexual violence, and copycat rapes and murders, Kubrick had *A Clockwork Orange* withdrawn in the UK, which meant that in a pre-YouTube world, none of the video's intended audience had any idea what it was based on. The film was finally re-released after the director's death in 1999, when this writer and his friends packed into the local multiplex to finally see what the video for The Universal was all about.

Typical of the campaign that surrounded *The Great Escape*, were Blur trying to be too clever for their own good? After all, who was it that was buying their records. Kids, when they wanted it to be adults. There is little doubt that The Universal is one of their strongest tracks as a band, but the fact it wasn't perhaps released in the right way left the whole story around it, again, slightly out of synch with itself.

UK Official Singles Chart – Top 10 – 19th November 1995:

1. I Believe/Up on the Roof – Robson & Jerome
2. Gangsta's Paradise – Coolio ft. L.V.
3. Missing – Everything but The Girl
4. Wonderwall – Oasis
5. **The Universal – Blur**
6. You'll See – Madonna
7. Anywhere Is – Enya
8. Father and Son – Boyzone
9. It's Oh So Quiet – Björk
10. Lie to Me – Bon Jovi

As 1995 drew slowly towards its end, we can yet again see a top 10 packed with songs that would go on to stand the test of time, including Björk's biggest commercially successful single, It's Oh So Quiet. Our old friends Robson & Jerome were at number 1 both in the singles and the albums chart, but putting them aside, with the modern hip-hop classic Gangsta's Paradise by Coolio at number 2, Missing by Everything but The Girl at 3 and Wonderwall at 4, it is perhaps inevitable that a single as subtle as The Universal only managed number 5. Perhaps Damon should have suggested moving the release date once more.

Reversal of Fortune – the end of 1995

After the spat with Oasis, alongside (or perhaps as a result of) the combative backlash against *The Great Escape*, the heinous accusation was levelled at Blur of being inauthentic and most worryingly, middle-class, and their stock immediately fell as a result. As with most of the band's praise and castigation, the majority of the fall-out was laid most prominently on Damon Albarn's shoulders. After all, he had near single-handedly invented Britpop and (miss-)managed the whole Battle of Britpop affair, why shouldn't he take the blame for what happened next? As Alex James said, "After being the People's Hero, Damon was the People's Prick for a short period...basically, he was a loser—very publicly."[xxi]

Whereas the Gallagher brothers, who had grown up in the impecunious Manchester suburb of Burnage, were presented as the classic working-class heroes that their idol John Lennon had sung about on his song of the same name (the B-side to Imagine in 1971). They wore their roots as a badge of honour, rising through the ranks to achieve world-wide success despite their onerous upbringing. "They've never had a paper round," said Noel Gallagher in the Britpop film *Live Forever* in 2003. "I had a milk round, I worked on building sites, that fundamentally makes my soul a lot more purer than theirs [Blur's]." Ouch!

Despite what Noel might say, accused of being middle-class on its own may not make you public enemy number one (not even in Britain), had Blur not chosen to trade on classic working-class commodities on *Parklife*. Notably on the title track, on which Londoner Phil Daniels speak-raps the lyrics in his thick, overly-pronounced, cockney accent. "Know what I mean!"

This may have never become of any relevance had the Battle of Britpop not caused a slew of overly analysed pieces by music writers, looking to high-light the differences between Blur and Oasis. So, when it was discovered that Damon was not in fact as cockney as *Parklife* may have given the impression of, accusations were donned of a forced 'mockney' moniker, of slumming it, and even of cultural appropriation.

It was a timely accusation, coming also in the wake of Pulp's hit single Common People. Released a few months earlier in May 1995, the song was by another authentic working-class band, and was about a rich international student from Greece who ascribed to finding glamour in the squalor, only to discover the truth was very far from the legend. The song reached number 2 in the UK Official Singles Chart and became the band's, and one of Britpop's, key anthems, leaving Damon and Blur victims of their own success. Albarn would later come to realise the mistakes he and the band made with *The Great Escape*, eventually saying in 2007, "I've made two bad records. The first record, which is awful, and *The Great Escape*, which was messy."[xxii]

On the episode of the Southbank Show about Blur, aired in 1999, Damon travels back to his secondary school, the Stanway Comprehensive, noting how (still ten years later) the conditions are so basic, the classrooms in disrepair. It pissed him off, he said, that the press made such a thing back in 1995 about him being middle-class, when he had been to comprehensive school, just like Oasis and Pulp. It is true that Blur are hardly as posh as Coldplay, Mumford and Sons or Keane, but as is so often the case with the British class system, it is much more complex than that. Damon had the support of artistic parents, who encouraged and supported him with music lessons and a place at drama college, Noel and Liam Gallagher had an alcoholic father who beat them and their mother, and a milk round.

Blur undoubtably made their own way in the music industry, just as Oasis did, and no-one was doubting that Damon was one of the country's most gifted songwriters, but what this inevitably meant was, that by the end of 1995, a year that should have seen Blur go stratospheric, they had stumbled, the press turning against them. With two singles still to release from *The Great Escape* in 1996, this difficult phase was far from over, but each of the band's members knew that something needed to change if they were to survive. They were certainly up that famous creek, but at least they had a paddle. The band's reaction was to go and make the best album of their career.

CHAPTER SIX
Eponymous Reinvention – Foreign Shores – "Woo hoo!" (1996-97)

Blur's last booking in 1995 was playing at the 12,500 capacity Wembley Arena on 16th December. Right next to London's 50,000 capacity Wembley Stadium, perhaps most famous for hosting Live Aid back in 1985. What should have been heralded as a triumphant homecoming in an arena setting could only be measured by its proximity to the mammoth stadium that it sat a stone's throw from. With arch rivals Oasis having played two nights at Earls Court to some 40,000 people just a few weeks earlier, the Wembley Arena show could only look like something of a come down for Blur, ending the year that, despite their continued success (*The Great Escape* was still selling very well), it must have felt like something had gone quite wrong.

The new year started with a tour of North America, playing Vancouver, before heading to Seattle (home place of the very grunge Blur had aimed to kill off in the UK), Portland, San Francisco, Los Angles, Denver, Dallas, Austin, Atlanta, St. Louis, Chicago, New York, Boston, and finally Washington. Their biggest go at North America yet. They were then briefly back in the UK for the release of their next single Stereotypes, before heading off to Europe until the end of March. Plans for recording the follow up to *The Great Escape* were forming, with the band keen to clear the air and move on as swiftly as they could. For the first time, it seemed that the influences for whatever that album would look like would come not from Britain but from the very place that they had been rallying so hard against all these years: America.

Single 14:

Stereotypes
Released: 12th February 1996; UK Chart Position: 7;
Label: Food; Album: *The Great Escape*
B-sides: UK version: The Man Who Left Himself; Tame; Ludwig
International version: The Horrors; A Song; St. Louis
Producer: Stephen Street

UK Official Singles Chart – Top 10 – 18th February 1996:

1. Spaceman – Babylon Zoo
2. Anything – 3T
3. Children – Robert Miles
4. I Got 5 on It – Luniz
5. Lifted – Lighthouse Family
6. One of Us – Joan Osborne
7. **Stereotypes – Blur**
8. Hyperballad – Björk
9. I Just Want to Make Love to You – Etta James
10. I Wanna Be a Hippie – Technohead

The week that Stereotypes reached number 7, the albums chart was jam packed with the likes of Oasis, M People, Alani Morrissette, Radiohead, Pulp, Paul Weller; and Britpoppers the Bluetones were even at number 1 with their debut album *Expecting to Fly*, so it was clear to see exactly where the nation's head was at.

In the singles chart, the phenomenon that was Spaceman by Babylon Zoo was riding high at number 1 for the fifth week in the row. The song, made famous because of its use in a Levi's TV advert, was the biggest selling single of the year, and made a very brief star out of

Jas Mann, before the one hit wonder outfit disappeared without a trace.

All eight singles released by Oasis were in the top 100, whilst alongside Stereotypes, only The Universal hung on at 99. Reaching number 7 was a solid effort for Blur, but those Oasis comparisons were going nowhere fast, and Damon Albarn was discovering that every time he was out in public people would blast Roll With It from their bedroom windows, shop doorways or public houses. Luckily, he was on tour for much of it, and by the time he did return, it was obvious to see why he chose to buy a house in Iceland.

Before that though, there was one more single to be released from *The Great Escape*.

Single 15:

Charmless Man
Released: 29th April 1996; UK Chart Position: 5; Label: Food; Album: *The Great Escape*
B-sides: UK version: The Horrors; A Song; St. Louis
International version: The Man Who Left Himself; Tame; Ludwig
Producer: Stephen Street

UK Official Singles Chart – Top 10 – 5th May 1996:

1. Fastlove – George Michael
2. Return of the Mack – Mark Morrison
3. Ooh Aah…Just a Little Bit – Gina G
4. Cecilia – Suggs & Louchie Lou/Michie One
5. **Charmless Man – Blur**
6. Move Move Move (The Red Tribe) – 1996 Man Utd FA Cup Squad
7. Cut Some Rug/Castle Rock – The Bluetones

8. Woo-hah!! Got You All in Check – Busta Rhymes
9. A Design for Life – Manic Street Preachers
10. Klubbhopping – Klubbheads

Charmless Man went straight in at a respectable number 5 in the singles chart, spending just eight weeks on the chart before disappearing for good, and with it, the end of *The Great Escape* campaign, which for good or bad had certainly changed things for Blur.

At number 9 that week was the first new music from Welsh band Manic Street Preachers since 1994's *The Holy Bible*. Having peaked at number 2, two weeks earlier (stopped from reaching the top spot by Mark Morrison's pop classic Return of the Mack), A Design for Life is today, the Manics most famous song. It signalled a complete turnaround in style and fortune for a band who had dramatically changed their penchant for writing intense, macabre songs about anorexia and child exploitation, into this positive working-class hymn about the power of solidarity. Though they had previously rejected Britpop, they were all too happy to use the prominence of the musical movement to reposition their career. By the end of the century the Manics would be the biggest band in Britain.

As previously discussed, by this point Blur were used to releasing two editions of their singles, meaning there were a total of six new tracks for every new single release, quite an effort for any band. However, Stereotypes and Charmless Man, were each put out with alternate track listing, the UK and international editions being swapped around, so realistically, there was only one track listing per release.

B-sides are an important outlet for a band because they are a chance for them to try out new material without having the pressure of the song being analysed the way singles and album tracks are. Also, with the A-side often having been written and recorded up to a year before release, B-sides are also an opportunity for the band to showcase examples of where their heads are at in the now. This is most clearly defined on tracks like The Man Who Left Himself, and Tame. Showcasing their influences once more, the latter song borrows its title from track 2 of the classic Pixies album *Doolittle*, and whilst it is still clearly Blur, it also has a loose, post-grungey feel, with a beautifully dirgy fuzz guitar line from Graham Coxon, and whirring keyboard part that would not have been out of place on an album by the American band Pavement, who as we'll come to see, were to be a huge influence on Blur's next album.

These B-sides signalled that perhaps the days of social commentary on charmless men and wife-swappers were numbered, and the feel and tone of the band's sound would once again become the most important aspect. Lyrically too, Albarn was to move away from looking at the world around him and focus instead on what most songwriters focus on: matters of the heart.

As it would turn out, Blur's next album was going to be another huge step forward for the band. However, rather than defining the state of the nation sound as they did with *Parklife*, Blur would be one of a small but valid contingent of bands that would release serious, grown-up records in 1997, prompting a lurch forward in musical style and development in sound, one that marked Blur out from many of their contemporaries.

Blur was a direct reaction to the disposable records pumped out during the Britpop years from the likes of the Bluetones, Shed Seven, Sleeper, Menswear, Dodgy, Geneva, Echobelly, Cast and the Longpigs, all down-the-line indie-rock acts with listenable enough songs, but perhaps without a distinct enough identity of their own. Shed Seven, the Bluetones and Sleeper would all release lacklustre albums in 1997 and 1998 that would bring about the end of their respective careers. Menswear didn't even get to release their second album. Blur's decision to yet again push against what was expected of them, proved they still had their metaphorical finger on the pulse, and that the UK music scene was looking to develop once more, and that the damp squib that Britpop had become, was well past its sell by date.

At the same time that Blur were recording what would become *Blur*, Spirtualized were recording their third album, the psychedelic post-rock classic *Ladies and Gentleman We Are Floating in Space*; Radiohead were recording the era-defining *OK Computer*; and the negative to Oasis' positive, The Verve, were about to start work on what would become their own opus, the mega-hit *Urban Hymns*.

Those sat in the wings taking notes included Travis, whose Oasis-lite work on their 1997 debut album *Good Feeling* was about to be ousted in favour of an album of simple yet serious songs that would make up 1999's *The Man Who;* a pre-U2 phase Coldplay, those 2000 debut album *Parachutes* was filled with introspective minor-chord ballads about breakups, paranoia and not fitting in; and Snow Patrol, who would combine both of these bands output on their cross over 2002 third album *Final Straw,* and its mega hit, Run.

The most highly anticipated album since *Sgt. Peppar's Lonely Hearts Club Band*, Oasis' 1997 third album *Be Here Now*, managed to appear both unnecessarily pompous and superficially dated in comparison.

That's Why Damon's Gone to Iceland

Damon Albarn first came up with the idea of buying a house in the Icelandic capital of Reykjavik in March 1996. He and partner Justine Frischmann had been living in the huge Westbourne Grove Victorian town house that Frischmann's wealthy father had bought her, for two years, and due to the immense pressure of public attention, combined with the fact that Justine's band Elastica were experiencing success in America, the couple were kept on the road for most of that year and Albarn was mostly alone in Westbourne Grove, fuelling his solitude further.

Albarn's new home from home was in the central Reykjavik district of Laugardalshöll, where on 8th September 1996 Blur would play their new material live for the first time. He quickly fell in with the local musical talent, befriending Einar Örn Benediktsson, from Iceland's most famous indie-rock band the Sugarcubes. The band, who sang in English, had been signed to the London based indie label One Little Indian and had reached the top 20 in the UK charts with their debut album *Life's Too Good* in 1988. The band had not long split, and their former singer Björk was by now world famous for her solo work, after the huge crossover success of her first solo album *Debut* and its single Play Dead, produced by David Arnold (best known for scoring a handful of James Bond films), in 1993, and who had just scored her biggest worldwide hit with It's Oh So Quiet.

Drawing influence from a lot of the same musical styles, namely British post-punk bands such as Wire and Magazine, as well as a newly developing love of electronica, Albarn and Benediktsson went on to make music together, composing and recording the soundtrack to the 2000 Icelandic independent film *101 Reykjavik*, directed by Baltasar Kormákur, who would go on to have success in Hollywood with *Everest* in 2015. *101 Reykjavik* is a coming of age black comedy centred on the story of a young Icelandic man falling for his mother's female Spanish lover, and the mainly electronic soundtrack showcased a new side to Albarn's musical life that was soon to be explored further with his Gorillaz side-project the following year in 2001.

Back in London, the need for separation from their lives was also true of the other members of Blur. Alex James' playboy lifestyle had developed to such a stage that he would later recall spending £1 million on champagne alone during this time, and his continued residence at the Soho Club as well as the release of his flowery yet hollow side project Me Me Me's top twenty single Hanging Around, was annoying the other band members. Coxon in particular had always been very vocal about his hatred for the fickle, disposable world of parties and socialites so common to the music industry and he too indulged his thirst for alcohol, but in a remarkably different way to James, preferring to slum it in the local pubs of Camden hanging out with the "painters and decorates"[xxiii] who he felt had more depth than the superficial hangers-on in the music industry.

Dave Rowntree on the other hand had quit drinking for a year by early 1996, a fact that itself spoke volumes about what he considered to be at the root of a lot of the band's issues. The others didn't seem to notice, or if they did, chose not to comment.

With each of the once tight-knit group pulling in starkly different directions, it became quickly apparent that whatever the new album was going to sound like, it was going to be decidedly different to their previous output. Damon and Graham even struck up a postal correspondence, in which Coxon stated he wanted to make music "to scare people again".[xxiv]

Blur's early mantra had been around wishing to rid the world of grunge, so when they began to embrace a distortion heavy guitar, fuzz-bass, pounding drum sound on their new material it may well have appeared as if they were exploiting the very music they claimed to hate. However, it wasn't grunge that they were listening to, but in fact another side to the American independent scene, with Coxon drawing the group's attention to Sonic Youth, Dinosaur Jr., The Sebadoh, The Breeders, Throwing Muses and most prominently, Pavement. Although these groups shared a similar style to Nirvana, Soundgarden and the other grunge bands there was an element of sensitivity to their music, which made their music less controversial, and more introspective. These groups are not lumped together in any kind of a scene, but it was this overall idea of lo-fi music made for oneself, rather than as a saleable commodity, that interested Coxon, and then the rest of the band.

Pavement had begun their existence as an underground indie rock band from California in the late nineteen eighties. They combined lilting acoustic led melodies with huge roughly hewn guitars and nothing in-between. Out went the sweet major chords popularised by The Beatles, Dylan and The Byrds, in favour of awkward sounding chords strummed on battered acoustic guitars with names like EmSUS11add9, or electric guitars purposefully tuned against what was expected. The result was the familiar layered with the Avant Garde, like a painting by Van Gogh or a novel by Graham Greene, where the world appears at first to be normal, but on closer inspection is in fact out of kilter. This has the effect of being both disorientating and thrilling, ultimately making sense within the confines of its own world.

This approach fits in with the ethos championed by Neil Young and Crazy Horse that the feeling of a song, and the passion of the performance, is much more important than technical proficiency. But it also has the effect of distancing the listener from the overly sentimental lyrical content, avoiding mawkishness at all costs. So, once again drawing on the work of Berthold Brecht.

Alex James however wasn't so sure about this change of sound. He said about Pavement: "'I didn't like that archness; pretending to be bad musicians…They sounded like a sixth form band to me.'"[xxv] James was out-voted though and after Pavement lead singer and chief songwriter Stephen Malkmus lived briefly at Albarn and Frischmann's place in 1996, the group decision was made to "let Graham off the leash"[xxvi] and Blur *Blur* was underway.

The first new material to surface did so on the tour of America in early 1996, supported by The Rentals, who had something of a minor hit in the American Billboard Top 100 in 1995 with Friends of P. Damon Albarn in particular was quite taken with the band and soon presented Blur with two new songs which wore their new influences proudly. One of them was called Chinese Bombs and sounded just like the material that Seymour had once upon a time revelled in. The other neither had a proper name nor any proper lyrics, but eventually became known simply at Song 2 due to its positioning on the album. The fuzz bass on Friends of P. sounds remarkably similar to the one that Alex James would soon make famous the world over when Song 2 accidentally became Blur's biggest ever release.

Recording for the new record began at Mayfair Studios in Primrose Hill in June 1996, and at first things got off to a typical start, with the band filling their ten-hour days layering Damon's pre-composed material, just as they had always done. Before long though, they started to jam together for the first time as a unit, quickly realising that the years they had been playing together gave them an ingrained intuition, and the songs soon took on wholly different lives of their own.

Stephen Street had bought to the sessions a RADAR (Random Access Digital Audio Recorder). A digital multitrack recorder capable of recording and playing back twenty-four tracks of audio. This meant that he could let the band play and then edit it up later, rather than having to use a set amount of tape. The change gave bands the luxury of near infinite takes, or in this case, long freeform jams that could later be spliced up and put back together.

Neither did the band demo any of the tracks. In most cases, what is heard on the record is how the songs were written. This is what gives the album its freer, more open sound, and meant that the band's focus developed away from writing hit singles, and more toward creating material for themselves. Little consideration was given to which songs would be the singles, and the band allowed themselves to indulge the jazz musicians' instinct to create through prolonged improvisation.

Needing to escape the UK, and Albarn's fame, Damon and Street decamped to Reykjavik in late August 1996 with the intention of editing and mixing what they thought was the finished record, before they called for the rest of the band to join them. Things started to come alive in the new setting and the band made the most of the fact that as the year bore on it was dark for nearly twenty hours a day, the band using the near perpetual night-time to fuel their creativity. Just like potatoes, rock musicians grow much better in the dark.

Iceland can be thanked for the album's sparseness, which was specifically sought by the band, after the layered extravagance of *The Great Escape* and *Parklife*. Wishing to reset the clock, the band did not want anything on the record not performed by the four members, and in support of this they decided to appear live at the five thousand capacity Laugardalshöll arena on 8th September 1996, just the four of them, at very short notice. They played a mammoth twenty-three song set, including three new songs, notably Beetlebum, which by this point had been chosen as the first single from the album.

The album was finally finished in November 1996 with Beetlebum slated for release in late January 1997. Initially radio wouldn't touch it, Andy Ross and Food Records were reluctant to release it, the industry thinking that the band had strayed too far from audience expectations. But, just as *The Great Escape* had changed the public opinion about the band, now the pendulum was due for an almighty swing back in their favour, and the single went straight in at number 1.

Single 16:

Beetlebum
Released: 20th January 1997; UK Chart Position: 1;
Label: Food; Album: *Blur*
B-sides: CD1: All your Life; A Spell (For Money)
CD2: Beetlebum (Mario Caldato Jr. mix); Woodpigeon Song; Danehall
Producer: Stephen Street

UK Official Singles Chart – Top 10 – 26th January 1997:

1. **Beetlebum – Blur**
2. Your Woman – White Town
3. Older/I Can't Make You Love Me – George Michael
4. Nancy Boy – Placebo
5. Where Do You Go – No Mercy
6. Say What You Want – Texas
7. Walk on By – Gabrielle
8. Professional Widow (It's Got to be Big) – Tori Amos
9. Remember Me – Blueboy
10. Don't Let Go (Love) – En Vogue

It was a relatively slow week for music when Beetlebum hit the shelves, and with no other act in the top 10 in quite the same bracket as Blur, it made number 1 comfortably. This is not to downplay the song's strength, it is to this day one of the band's strongest compositions and most popular tracks, typifying the band's reinvention, but also that of British music immediately post-Britpop.

The change in mood was also represented by the single straight in at number 4 that week, the fourth single from the British/American/European cross-pollinated/pan-sexual indie-rock act Placebo, with their most well-known single, Nancy Boy. Led by the androgynous, sexually ambiguous lead singer and guitarist Brian Molko, the band took up where Suede had left off with tracks like Animal Lover and Animal Nitrate, exploring themes on their material of sexual misadventures and drug abuse. The popularity of their self-named 1997 debut album, and its 1998 follow up *Without You I'm Nothing*, and its huge lead single Pure Morning, worked at pushing against the heteronormative aspects so typical to British music in the late nineties.

He's on It

Despite Andy Ross' reticence, his instinct to trust his band was immediately rewarded and Beetlebum was immediately heralded for embracing a much more sophisticated sound for Blur.

Noel Gallagher would later admit to hearing the song and kicking himself because he thought it was so good. The praise is fitting, Damon had purposefully set out to beat Oasis at their own game and try and write a song that the Beatles would have recorded if they were around in 1997. Stephen Thomas Erlewine says on AllMusic, "'Beetlebum' runs through [The Beatles'] *White Album* in the space of five minutes"[xxvii]. Albarn said, "I want Noel to listen to Beetlebum and realise that it is… closer [to The Beatles than Oasis]"[xxviii].

Album 5:

Blur
Released: 10th February 1997; UK Chart Position: 1; Label: Food
Track Listing: Beetlebum; Song 2; Country Sad Ballad Man; M.O.R. (Albarn, Coxon, James, Rowntree, Bowie, Eno); On Your Own; Theme From Retro;

You're So Great; Death of a Party; Chinese Bombs; I'm Just a Killer for Your Love; Look Inside America; Strange News from Another Star; Movin' On; Essex Dogs
Producer: Stephen Street

UK Official Albums Chart – Top 10 – 16th February 1997:

1. ***Blur* – Blur**
2. *White on Blonde* – Texas
3. *Spice* – Spice Girls
4. *Evita* – OST – Madonna
5. *The Smurfs Hits '97* – Vol. 1 – Smurfs
6. *Blue is the Colour* – Beautiful South
7. *Glow* – Reef
8. *Ocean Drive* – Lighthouse Family
9. *Tragic Kingdom* – No Doubt
10. Older – George Michael

Eponymous Reinvention

In many ways *Blur* is Blur's coming of age record. The name itself suggests year zero, they are pressing the reset button and starting again. This is also true of the band's decision to jam for the first time, and the newly employed space to the album is immediately apparent. Had they not let themselves create the songs as they played them, would the album have had the beautifully elongated coda to Beetlbum, for example? Which after Albarn's laconic repeated calls of 'he's on it', is resolutely in place for the final minute and six seconds of the track. This piece of music consists simply of a signature Coxon echo-drenched repeated guitar lick over the song's same rhythm track, with some additional indecipherable scratchy radio sample lines, but somehow lays claim to be one of the finest moments of the band's existence.

Thematically, there is an overarching melancholia felt on the album's lyrics which is evident in the song titles: On Your Own, Movin' On and Country Sad Ballad Man (how sad? *Country* sad) speak for themselves, whilst M.O.R. tells the story of how Albarn felt Blur's music had become middle of the road, whilst Look Inside America says in words just what the album was asking the listener to do musically. Just as London Loves had done on *Parklife*. Damon had not completely abandoned his voyeuristic look at contemporary life, he was just aiming the focus at himself.

"I think Beetlebum's representative of the fact that as the band's got older, the songs have become more simple," said Alex James. "Now we can play them with a lot more feeling."[xxix] The song itself is relatively simple to play. However, it is far from rudimentary, and employs the same tactic The Beatles did with Come Together and many of the songs on *Abbey Road* (mostly the Lennon composed ones): the simplicity of the chord sequence offering the highly experienced band the opportunity of layering their own style over the top. Alex James provides one of his trademark rolling bass lines once the rhythm section joins in halfway through the verse, and Rowntree's solid beat and accompanying tambourine roots the band back within the immediately identifiable indie-rock sound, ensuring they haven't distanced themselves too much. The song becomes all about the style and not about the complexity.

This in itself is nothing new for the band. Most of their songs follow simple chord sequences and a 4/4 time signature, but as the great jazz drummer (and full-time lunatic) Ginger Baker said of his supergroup Cream, "It didn't matter what the song was. It was the people that played it that made it."[xxx] Damon understood this and made sure when composing the songs on *Blur* to leave space for the band to add their own individuality on top, therefore taping into the very essence of the band.

Lyrically the song is about his relationship with Frischmann. As a Beatles fan she is the 'Beetle-bum' of the title. The song is far from romantic though, the lyric being partly about the physical affect she has upon him: "She'll suck your thumb, She'll make you cum", but mostly being about her decent into heroin abuse, and the subsequent distance this caused in their relationship. He uses the song's theme of the negative implications of drug addiction as a metaphor for how he feels about his relationship with her. He is addicted to her like she is addicted to heroin, and can't give her up, even if he wanted to.

Single 17:

Song 2
Released: 7th April 1997; UK Chart Position: 2; Label: Food; Album: *Blur*
B-sides: CD1: Get Out of Cities; Polished Stone
CD2: Bustin' + Dronin; Country Sad Ballad Man (live – acoustic)
Producer: Stephen Street

UK Official Singles Chart – Top 10 – 13th April 1997:

1. I Believe I Can Fly – R Kelly
2. **Song 2 – Blur**
3. The Saint – Orbital
4. Bellissima – DJ Quicksilver
5. Ready or Not – Course
6. Don't Speak – No Doubt
7. You Might Need Somebody – Shola Ama

8. MFEO – Kavana
9. Lazy – Suede
10. Halo – Texas

With R Kelly riding high at number 1 with his mega hit I Believe I Can Fly, dance outfit Orbital at 3 with the theme song to *The Saint* reboot, plus DJ Quicksilver, other forms of music were starting to filter into the Britpop obsessed charts as 1997 began to get going. That said, No Doubt's Don't Speak (down from number 1), their most radio-friendly song, was imported from the USA, and rock-pop band Texas were at number 10 with the Halo, the second single from their fourth (and by far their biggest) album *White on Blonde*, highlighting how groups were taking the indie approach to finding success.

Just outside the top 10, Supergrass were at 11 (down from 2 a week earlier – second place also to I Believe I Can Fly), with the first single from their second album in *It for the Money*, Richard III. Trying to distance themselves from the Monkees-esque moniker that mega-hit Alright had given them back in 1995, Richard III was a huge, dark, loud, rock belter, again hinting at the darker way that British indie-rock music was headed (helped along by the likes of Blur) as 1997 progressed.

Woo Hoo!

Perhaps they should have called it Song 1 and it would have gone to the top spot, but its chart positioning aside, the cult of Song 2 hit the band completely unexpectedly, becoming the band's biggest release totally by accident, eventually netting them some £2 million[xxxi] in the process. To put it in perspective, at time of writing, Song 2 has 365 million plays on Spotify, Blur's second most streamed song is Girls & Boys, which has 93 million plays.

Where Beetlebum worked hard to showcase a deeper more introspective side to the band, the disposable lyrical content to Song 2 threatened to reverse this with one mistimed lyric about heads being checked by jumbo-jets. But where many of the band's songs had been made up of nonsensical lyrics and so taken on a subsequent cartoon image before, track two on *Blur* somehow managed to avoid this association and instead became known for its fuzz bass, its quiet-quiet-loud guitars and its chanted chorus that gave rise to the prominence of the ubiquitous phrase of joy: "Woo hoo!"

Given the American influence on the album the song was originally taken as a parody of grunge, aping the jangly guitar followed by distortion and pounding drum intro of Nirvana's Smells Like Teen Spirit, but after the song crossed over into the mainstream, finding its way onto the Billboard Top 200 in America, the intent soon palled in comparison to the song's significance on its own terms. Song 2 very quickly became itself, and has existed in the world ever since, having never dropped off commercial radio playlists, TV adverts about anything containing high octane adventure, and featuring in the set list of sixth-form school bands, in the twenty-odd years since it was originally released.

The band, knowing that they were long enough in the tooth not to become dwarfed by it, must have been not the least bit amused that it was Song 2 rather than Beetlebum that was nominated for Best British Single at the 1998 Brit Awards (it lost out to Never Ever by All Saints). And that it ended up being the band's representative on the track list for the *Music of the Millennium* compilation CD, released jointly by Virgin, Universal and EMI in 2000, sitting alongside Imagine by John Lennon, Candle in the Wind by Elton John, No Woman No Cry by Bob Marley and of course Wonderwall by Oasis.

Single 18:

On Your Own
Released: 16th June 1997; UK Chart Position: 5; Label: Food; Album: *Blur*
B-sides: CD1: Popscene; Song 2; On Your Own
CD2: Chinese Bombs; Movin' On; M.O.R.
(all B-sides recorded live at John Peel's house Peel Acres)
Producer: Stephen Street

UK Official Singles Chart – Top 10 – 22nd June 1997:

1. I'll Be Missing You – Puff Daddy & Faith Evans
2. Bitter Sweet Symphony – The Verve
3. MMM Bop – Hanson
4. Hundred Mile High City – Ocean Colour Scene
5. **On Your Own - Blur**
6. I Wanna Be the Only One – Eternal ft. Bebe Winans
7. Free – Ultra Nate
8. Nothing Lasts Forever – Echo and the Bunnymen
9. Guiding Star – Cast
10. Coco Jamboo – Mr President

Despite Britpop's dominance on the charts having just over a year left on its tenure, June 1997 saw some of the finest indie-rock anthems spreading themselves across the top 10, with the first single from Ocean Colour Scene's third album *Marchin' Already*, heading straight to number 4; the second single from Cast's second album *Mother Nature Calls* at number 9; and the modern classic Bitter Sweet Symphony by The Verve just being pipped to the post by the ode to fallen heroes that was Puff Daddy's Police lift off, I'll Be Missing You. With such strong singles it is perhaps obvious why Blur only reached number 5 with the third single from *Blur*, On Your Own. The song is one of the strongest on the album, but as people already owned it, they would perhaps rather buy Bitter Sweet Symphony with their pocket money.

Outside the top 10, Primal Scream were at number 16 with their own twist on Britpop, Star, from their return to form album *Vanishing Point*; The Charlatans were at 24 with How High and Supergrass were at 29 with Sun Hits the Sky. A very strong week for single releases.

On Your Own is one of Coxon's greatest guitar riffs. It shows how his use of guitar effects came to define his style as a guitar player. On the track he uses the lesser known Gonkulator Modulator pedal, which combines "a Grunge style distortion with a ring modulator"[xxxii], giving it that strange computerised feel.

Stephen Street later said that Coxon plays the guitar with his feet, to which Coxon said in 2017, "Really, my guitar playing is effects playing…I went to the guitar via pedals, to excite me." And only on *Blur* was he really afforded the opportunity of employing this skill prominently for the first time. He added in 2017, "Damon was a good enabler for me to become noisy that time [on *Blur*]. He wrote these short fast things for me to go berserk on, as a sort of reward"[xxxiii].

Single 19:

M.O.R. (Albarn, Coxon, James, Rowntree, Bowie, Eno)
Released: 15th September 1997; UK Chart Position: 15; Label: Food; Album: *Blur*
B-sides: Swallows in the Heatwave; Movin' On (Williams Orbit remix); Beetlebum (Moby's remix)
Producer: Stephen Street

UK Official Singles Chart – Top 10 – 21st September 1997:

1. Something About the Way You Look Tonight/Candle in the Wind – Elton John
2. Sunchyme – Dario G
3. Tubthumping – Chumbawamba
4. The Drugs Don't Work – The Verve
5. Men in Black – Will Smith
6. You Have Been Loved EP – George Michael
7. FIX – Blackstreet
8. Samba De Janeiro – Bellini
9. Never Gonna Let You Go – Tina Moore
10. (Un, Dos, Tres) Maria – Ricky Martin

....

15. M.O.R. – Blur

The first Blur single not to reach the top 10 since End of the Century three years earlier, M.O.R., or 'middle of the road', was the last single released from *Blur*. The skeleton of the song is composed around another simple chord sequence: D, E, B♭, D, which again leaves space for one of Coxon's most incendiary guitar riffs, but led to controversy due to the song's similarity to David Bowie's Boys Keep Swinging, from 1979's *Lodger* album (produced by Brian Eno).

The use of Bowie's melody aside, the lyric is Albarn telling the listener how middle of the road he feels his band's music had become:

It's automatic
I need to unload
Under the pressure
Gone middle of the road
Fall into fashion
Fall out again
We stick together

'Cause it never ends

This is Albarn's first lyric to explore the negative affect the last few years of fame have had upon his song writing, and how he feels the pressure to produce hit singles had pushed the band's material toward the middle of the road. In line with such exalted M.O.R. acts as Wings, ELO and possibly even ABBA.

The Return to Form

When the last single from *Blur*, M.O.R., was released, the band were a few dates into their biggest American tour to date, having come via the European festival season and dates in Greenland and Damon's second home, Reykjavík. Support on the North American tour, that took in some twenty dates, came from indie darlings The Dandy Warhols, the transatlantic, self-proclaimed outsiders, who were experiencing some success with their second album *Come Down*, and its tongue-in-dirty-cheek lead single Not If You Were the Last Junkie on Earth ("I never thought you'd be a junkie because heroin is so passe"), quite a far cry from the likes of Sleeper, who supported them during the *Parklife* tour. By October the band were heading east, first to Korea, then Australia, New Zealand, Thailand, Singapore, and Ireland, finally ending the year with an arena tour around the UK.

The nine-month world tour may have been driven by the success of Song 2 around the world, but the consensus was that the *Blur* album had put the band back on top. Repositioning themselves to create something that no-one ever would have expected from the band who sang Country House.

As 1998 began though, the band did something that they had never done before. They released an album of remixes of the tracks on *Blur*. Done by the likes of Moby (not far away from the phenomenal success of his own album *Play*), Thurston Moore from US noise-smiths Sonic Youth, dub expert Adrian Sherwood, and of course producer William Orbit, who was finding mega-success by reinventing Madonna (again) with her 1998 *Ray of Light* album. Blur liked Orbit's work so much they asked him to produce what would become their sixth studio album, *13* in 1999, finally cutting the ties with Stephen Street.

Remix Album:

Bustin' + Dronin'
Released: 25th February 1998; UK Chart Position: 50 [import only]; Label: Food
Track Listing: Disc 1: Movin' On" (Orbit); Death of a Party (Sherwood); On Your Own (Orbit); Beetlebum (Moby); Essex Dogs (Moore); Death of a Party (Orbit); Theme From Retro (McEntire); Death of a Party (Sherwood); On Your Own (Orbit)
Disc 2: Popscene; Song 2; On Your Own; Chinese Bombs; Movin' On; M.O.R. (recorded live at Peel Acres)
Producers: William Orbit, Moby, Thurston Moore, John McEntire, Adrian Sherwood

The album, released as a Japanese important only, and so only reaching number 50 in the albums chart, showcased yet another side of the band. A side that was interested in experimenting even more than they had done on the likes of Essex Dogs, and one that was interested in embracing dub and electro just as much as they were solid rock 'n' roll. After the joys of the new side of the band seen on *Blur*, *Bustin' + Dronin'* helped to showcase the fact that the school boy punks were long gone, and in their place were the serious musicians looking to develop as far away from Country House and Damien Hirst as they possibly could.

They had bounced back better than Lazarus, and as 1998 bore on and the band headed into their own purpose built studio in June (really testing their luck, they called it 13), emerging only to play a handful of live dates, most notably a headline slot at that year's Glastonbury Festival on Saturday 27th June. They hunkered down until October, recording what would become *13*, their most experimental, alternative and noisy, yet resolutely tuneful and exciting record to date. One that would, lyrically, soundtrack the final massive implosion of Damon Albarn's relationship with Justine Frischmann.

CHAPTER SEVEN
End of the Century/End of an Affair – *13* and Onwards (1999-00)

Almost exactly a year after *Bustin' + Dronin'* had helped bridge the gap between *Blur* and *13*, as well as signal yet another new direction for the band, a new single finally came in the form of the epic Tender. And what a new single it was. With the rhythm section consisting of Alex James playing an upright double bass, and Dave Rowntree hammering together bits of plywood, Graham Coxon taking the lead vocal on the chorus and the London Community Gospel Choir filling out the backing vocals, it was immediately clear that at nearly eight minutes long, Tender was not like any Blur single, or any other single in the charts at the time. It was a simple twist of chart fate, and a seventeen-year-old girl from Mississippi, that kept it from the top spot.

Single 19:

Tender
Released: 22nd February 1999; UK Chart Position: 2; Label: Food; Album: *13*
B-sides: CD1: All We Want; Mellow Jam
CD2: French Song; Song 2; Song 2 (video)
Producer: William Orbit (Tender, Mellow Jam and French Song); Stephen Street (All We Want and Song 2)

UK Official Singles Chart – Top 10 – 28th February 1999:

1. Baby One More Time – Britney Spears
2. **Tender – Blur**
3. It's Not Right But It's Ok – Whitney

Houston

4. Just Looking – Stereophonics
5. Strong Enough – Cher
6. Runaway – Corrs
7. Erase/Rewind – Cardigans
8. Fly Away – Lenny Kravitz
9. Lullaby – Shawn Mullins
10. Written in the Stars – Elton John & Leann Rimes

With seven of the top 10 singles, new releases that week, at least new music was finding its feet in a post-Britpop, pre-end of the millennium environment, that was struggling to find any real sense of identity. Any other week and Blur would have been number 1, but the modern classic pop anthem Hit Me Baby One More Time hung on to the top spot on its second week of release. The mega-hit would go on to have a clear 23 week run on the chart, signalling, alongside the likes of Whitney, Cher, and the Corrs, that pop music was back and about to experience something of a renaissance.

Britney would soon be joined in the charts by her ex-boyfriend Justin Timberlake, and another Mickey Mouse Club alumnus Christina Aguilera, each a smart pop act that would claim a spot at the top of the charts on both sides of the Atlantic with simple, singalong, R'n'B flavoured pop songs. The Corrs and the Cardigans would still include strummed acoustic guitars and synths of late nineties indie music, but they were now in the minority as the pendulum moved away from rock 'n' roll once more.

Not that Blur let this affect them at all, their new album *13* was soon to come out and prove that there was still a place for an imaginative, inventive rock band, when it became another huge album for the group.

Album Six:

13
Released: 15th March 1999; UK Chart Position: 1; Label: Parlophone
Track Listing: Tender (Albarn/Coxon); Bugman; Coffee & TV (Coxon); Swamp Song; 1992; B.L.U.R.E.M.I.; Battle; Mellow Song; Trailerpark; Caramel; Timm Trabb; No Distance Left to Run; Optigan 1
Producer: William Orbit

UK Official Albums Chart – Top 10 – 21st March 1999:

1. ***13* – Blur**
2. *Performance and Cocktails* – Stereophonics
3. *Talk on Corners* – Corrs
4. *I've Been Expecting You* – Robbie Williams
5. *Baby One More Time* – Britney Spears
6. *The Miseducation of* – Lauryn Hill
7. This is My Truth Tell Me Yours – Manic Street Preachers
8. *Forgiven, Not Forgotten* – Corrs
9. *Step One* – Steps
10. *Gran Turismo* – Cardigans

Despite the impending pop renaissance, 21st March 1999 consisted of a decidedly rock heavy top 10 for the albums chart, with Blur joined by the Stereophonics and Manic Street Preachers, two hugely successful bands, flying the flag for Wales' own renaissance of popular music. Similarly, indie-rock music influenced pop music was still evident with the likes of Robbie Williams and Cardigans, and two albums from the Irish brother/sister outfit the Corrs. Hints of the R'n'B that was on its way to dominate during the new millennium came in the form of former-Fugee Lauryn Hill, who was embarking on her enormously successful solo career; and purest pop in the form of Steps, whose ominously titled first album *Step One*, which everyone hoped was not the beginning of a twelve step programme.

It was fitting that Blur's new album reached number 1 the first week of its release. The new work, now distanced from the mid-nineties pop-fest of *Parklife* and *The Great Escape* by three years and a whole album, signalled that many British bands were trying something new and experimental, and were being rewarded by an audience that was proving itself to be more discerning than many of the record companies may have given it credit for.

Strangely, of all the Blur albums, it was *Leisure* that found its way back into the charts the week that *13* came out, climbing all the way to number 72, presumably there was a discount offer on in HMV.

13 – Lucky for Some

With just 13 tracks in the offing (of course), *13* is the rarest of things, a Blur album with the correct number of tracks. At its most basic, *13* could be seen as *Blur* part II, but it was by far the band's most sophisticated release to date. It is their *White Album*, with tracks such as Battle and Trimm Trabb every bit as tuneful and listenable as they are weird and experimental. The album was the band's clearest of accomplishments, building on the work of *Blur* to push them further away from their former guise of Britpop pinups, and into the world of British musical icons, all in the space of 65 minutes. With the release of the record people would no longer mention them in the same breath as Oasis, rather they had become another Radiohead, experimental but accessible. Blur had grown up and dragged British indie-rock with them.

As with nearly all Blur albums, track one was also the lead single and set the tone for what was to come. After the disco-tastic raucousness of Girls & Boys, the pomposity of Country House and the out-there-ness of Beetlebum, which had divided critics right up until the moment the band's fans had immediately loved it, all bets were off when it came to the lead single from a Blur album, and Tender was their boldest statement of intent yet. Evolving from a classic Graham Coxon jangly guitar riff, the song manages to position Coxon's lo-fi stylings alongside one of Damon's epic melodies. It was the first time the pair had co-written a Blur song and what a way to kick things off. With his debut solo album, *The Sky is Too High*, having shifted 100,000 copies by the end of 1998, Graham was clearly on a confidence boosted writing streak, and just like on *Blur*, Damon had decided to embrace the guitarist's musical ambitions, continuing to let him off the leash, and the result finds the two old friends meeting in the middle of their areas of strength.

Like all the truly great songs, Tender is incredibly simple to play, Damon strums an A major chord on his acoustic guitar whilst Dave pounds his planks of wood in the background. When Graham joins in with his "oh my baby" it's not about the three simple repeated words, but the feel of the lilting melody that rises and falls as the epic songs swells to its grand conclusion. Years later, when the band reformed in 2009, Graham described how incredible the feeling was of hearing the 100,000 strong audience at Glastonbury singing back those three words.

In many ways William Orbit seemed like the perfect evolution of producer for the band. His desire to embrace experimentation fit in with the band's own ambitions for their new record; but he was every bit as leftfield a choice for producer as he was the perfect fit. Where Stephen Street had proved himself the ultimate indie-rock producer before even working with Blur, Orbit had done nothing of the sort. Whilst Street was cutting his teeth with indie-icons The Smiths, Orbit was forming the electro-synth group Torch Song. As a producer, he was largely untested in the studio, having worked only on Beth Orton's solo album *Superpinkymandy* in 1993, before helping to reinvent Madonna with her *Ray of Light* album in 1998. But it was this otherness, this desire to push the boundaries and never play it safe, that attracted Damon et al. They had played it safe with *The Great Escape* back in 1995, and that had landed them in a heap of trouble. Pushing the boundaries seemed like the only sensible solution.

Track two, a strange hybrid of Song 2 and Jubilee, Bugman, is Seymour grown up. Sounding like The Ramones might if they had ingested a plateful of hash cakes. Orbit's whirrs and beeps build to a cacophony of noise that nearly falls apart as the song judders its way to a conclusion. Somehow the song is nearly five minutes long, which is incredibly strange considering it is all but over after three minutes. The band wouldn't usually go this strange this early on in an album, but this is no ordinary Blur album, and Bugman concludes with the band jamming, Coxon's fuzz guitar augmented by Damon's improvised calls of "space is the place" perhaps a sly reference to the producer's (adopted) surname.

Coffee and TV is Graham Coxon's song. Picked up from a chord sequence Albarn had been knocking about, Graham drew together the best elements of his lo-fi solo work and produced a fantastic Blur tune. The only single released not sung by Damon, Coffee and TV is Blur's best effort at radio-friendly Americana (it would that year feature on the soundtrack to *Cruel intentions*), the subject matter hinting at Graham's efforts to avoid the alcohol shaped depression that was threatening to overtake him by this point.

As the album progresses a certain sense of nostalgia begins to present itself. As the band all began to turn 30 around the time of recording, plus the impending end of the century, the world began to look just as much backwards as it did forwards. Track 5, 1992, spoke for itself, with a suggestive title that harks back to one of the worst years of the band's existence, the song is a distant cousin to Sing from *Leisure*, without Damon's staccato piano line. Alongside Bugman, the oddly named B.L.U.R.E.M.I. was a slice of proto-punk the band had championed in their really early days, and referenced their record label's parent company, the country's oldest label, EMI (Food Records was folded into EMI subsidiary Parlophone in 1999). Lyrically, the song is about Blur and their early days, slipping in and out of first and third person narrative:

Group using the loop
Of another pop group
Group shooting the hoop
And starving it up into the soup
'Cause I'm of regular features
And Adidas trainers
Completing the cycle
Teenage maniacs
Will bring it all back

Damon's sense of nostalgia came not only from turning the big 3-0, but also due to the biggest of shakeups to occur in his adult life, the split with long term girlfriend, Justine Frischmann. Much was made of the album being about the breakup, and that is undoubtedly true, but just how *Modern Life* was said to be about an inherent Britishness, *13* was nearly lost down the rabbit hole of being 'the break up album'. The album is so much more, but, is also the break up album. Tender is undoubtedly about the split ("tender is the touch of someone that you love too much"), as is Battle ("battle someone, oh"), and most emphatically Damon sings on Trailerpark, "Lost my girl to the Rolling Stones". But the clearest indicator of the acrimonious split is on the song's final single and penultimate track, No Distance Left to Run. Adele would later make her career out of pouring her heart into a song where the subject tries to appear magnanimous in defeat, wishing their former partner the best in their new life, and considering how drenched in heartbreak and despair No Distance Left to Run is, it would be easy to see where she got the idea.

As a break up song, the track isn't as self-indulgent as Prince's Nothing Compares 2 U, or as music-hall as Adele's Someone Like You (despite coming from a very similar place lyrically), and Graham Coxon's dirty distorted fuzz box guitar lick, drags it out of the realms of sentimentality that it would have been a shame to lose it to. Back to our old friend Brecht then, juxtaposing the music with the lyrics so you focus on the subject matter. Or nearly. The rhythm section provides a gentle jazz-lite backdrop to the song about loss and regret so perfect that it is as if they aren't playing at all.

It's over
You don't need to tell me
I hope you're with someone who makes you
feel safe in your sleeping tonight
I won't kill myself, trying to stay in your life
I got no distance left to run

It's truly heart-breaking stuff, and it was a bold decision by Damon to a) include the song on the album, b) release it as a single, and c) play it live many many times. Such an act ran the risk of appearing like he was appropriating his own feelings – if that's even possible – playing on his own misery in order to sell records. But as the lead singers of two of Britpop's biggest acts, the couple had lived their relationship under the close scrutiny of the indie-press, since day one. It therefore made sense that they split up in public too. "That relationship really crashed… it was a spectacularly sad end," said Damon in the aptly named documentary *No Distance Left to Run*, and everyone associated with the band, or those that read the music press, felt like they were part of it too, therefore giving Damon credence to lay out his melancholia for all to see.

The first example of this however, goes back to the track Never Here on Elastica's debut eponymous album. Where nearly every other track was a short, sharp slice of punk-rock, none of them clocking in over three minutes, Never Here took its time, running for four and a half minutes, its mournful melody telling tales of a lover whose presence is so all encompassing that you can't live without them around, despite how self-involved they are:

We were sitting in, waiting
And I told you my plan
You were far too busy writing
Rhymes that didn't scan
And you lent me your records
And I lent you an ear
Funny how it seems to me now
That you were never here
Never really here

But this album isn't just about Justine, and as the second half of crazy experimental tracks like Trailerpark and Caramel fade, the clap-along Trimm Trabb drags the album back into the here and the now. "That's just the way it is," says Damon, a well-worn phrase for rock 'n' roll, but one that he manages to make sound fresh, adding one of his insistent chant-alongs: "I got trim trabb like the flash boys have", before Graham's huge guitars launch into life. Blur albums tend to petter out, *13* announces its conclusion with some of its finest moments coming in the second half.

That said though, the band structure the album just like all of their others. The strong single to start and set the tone, the quirky second single in the first three. The weird ones beginning around tracks five and six, and Mellow Song is positioned somewhere in the middle as the intermission track the band were always so fond of including.

Similarly, the pathos felt across the album was not just provided by Damon and Justine. This was an incredibly difficult time for the band as a whole, and the feeling spread that the end of the century may well be bringing with it, the end of the band. As sophisticated and experimental as the album was, the band were sadly going through their darkest period with their interpersonal relationships. As the album was focused mostly around the band's jamming sessions, and then pieced together afterwards (more like creating a film, the album came alive in the editing suite), the fragility of their relationships with one another made for some thrilling moments, but was not sustainable longer term.

Single 20:

Coffee & TV (Coxon)
Released: 28th June 1999; UK Chart Position: 11; Label: Food; Album: 13
B-sides: CD1: Trade Stylee (Alex's Bugman remix); Metal Hip Slop (Graham's Bugman remix)
CD2: X-Offender (Damon's Bugman remix); Coyote (Dave's Bugman remix)
(the Europe CD and 12-inch vinyl include all of the Bugman remixes)
Producer: William Orbit

UK Official Singles Chart – Top 10 – 4th July 1999:

1. 9pm (Till I Come) – ATB
2. Wild Wild West – Will Smith
3. My Love is Your Love – Whitney Houston
4. Boom, boom, boom, boom!! – Vengaboys
5. Bring it all Back – S Club 7
6. Sometimes – Britney Spears
7. Viva La Radio – Lolly
8. If You Had My Love – Jennifer Lopez
9. That Don't Impress Me Much – Shania Twain
10. Beautiful Stranger – Madonna
11. **Coffee & TV – Blur**

"It is all over now," Damon Albarn told NME in May 1996. "We killed Britpop. We chopped it up and put it under the patio long ago."[xxxiv] Little did Damon know that the result of this move would mean a resurgence in the charts of purest pop music. The charts are perhaps where pop music should live, and with the likes of Britney Spears and Jennifer Lopez being joined by the old guard of Whitney Houston and Madonna, who were reinventing themselves, then the end of the millennium was shaping up to be a solid time for pop music.

Aside from Blur, the only other indie-rock acts featured in the singles chart in June 1999 were the one (or two) hit wonders Semisonic with Secret Smile, former Mercury Music Prize winners Gomez with Bring it On, Suede who were very much on their way out, with She's in Fashion, and a handful of American hangers on, such as Hole, Marilyn Manson, and the Red Hot Chilli Peppars.

Single 21:

No Distance Left to Run
Released: 15th November 1999; UK Chart Position: 14;
Label: Food; Album: 13
B-sides: CD1: Tender (Cornelius remix)
[Albarn/Coxon]; So You
CD2: Battle (UNKLE remix); Beagle 2; No Distance
Left to Run (video)
Producer: William Orbit

UK Official Singles Chart – Top 10 – 21st November 1999:

1. King of the Castle – Wamdue Project
2. The Millennium Prayer – Cliff Richard
3. She's the One/It's Only Us – Robbie Williams
4. Will 2K – Will Smith
5. If I Could Turn Back the Hands of Time – R Kelly
6. I Try – Macy Gray
7. Left Me Up – Geri Halliwell
8. Keep on Movin' – Five
9. Everytime/Ready or Not – A1
10. Why – Glamma Kid

…………………………………

14. No Distance Left to Run – Blur

Cliff Richard's single, his 144th, The Millennium Prayer, which set the lyrics of The Lord's Prayer against the music of Auld Lang Syne, was released the same day as No Distance Left to Run, and went straight to number 2, rising to number 1 for the next three weeks, before slipping to number 2 for Christmas 1999; remaining at number 2 for the following week, for that all important millennium moment. It was an epic effort from the old crooner, then in his fifth decade of releasing music. The song was his 14th number 1 UK single. Today Richard's has made history yet again for having top 5 singles in eight consecutive decades (I guess it would be hard for them to be non-consecutive).

With the re-re-release of Imagine peaking at number 3 behind him, it showed the position of nostalgia that the industry was trying to push on the record buying public as the twentieth century came to a close. The people though had other ideas and it was Westlife that were at number 1 for both Christmas 1999 and the millennium moment, with their covers of I Have a Dream/Seasons in the Sun. I Have a Dream was of course a cover of the ABBA song from 1979, so there was a built in nostalgia already in place to the band's material, but the market was youngsters, who were discovering the songs for the first time. The new was therefore aiming to supplant the old establishment, sort of. Equalling Cliff's achievement, Westlife have had 14 UK number 1 singles. Luckily for all concerned, The Beatles are still holding strong in the top spot, with 17.

What Next?

With *13* out there in the world, the general consensus was that Blur were strengthening their position as being back on top form. The NME and Melody Maker made it one of their albums of the year, as did Q, Rolling Stone and Select (the Britpop mag, not yet long for this world), with many publications calling it a masterpiece. It seems though that the developed sound came at something of a cost, with Graham Coxon's more amplified role, exacerbated by his excessive drinking, creating friction in the studio unlike any the band had experienced previously. As Dave Rowntree said of the recording in *No Distance Left to Run*:

"It was quite a sad process making it. People were not turning up to the sessions, or turning up drunk, being abusive and storming off."

Despite the album's achievements, it was definitely time for a break, but before that there was the small matter of a lengthy tour, one that culminated at Reading Festival on 31st August, at which the band announced that they would be playing a gig at the Electric Ballroom in Camden featuring just their B-sides (a total nightmare as it turned out), followed by an arena tour where they would play all of their singles in release order, itself supporting a mammoth tenth anniversary box set of all of these singles, and then a best-of in the new year.

All of this activity – combined with the fact that it all came together at the end of the century they had been singing about since 1994 – had the added impact of suggesting that perhaps the band were about to bow out gracefully, which given the recent friction, would have been no huge surprise.

In fact, they just took an extended break in which Damon began Gorillaz, Graham continued his solo outings, Alex retreated to his farm to make cheese, and Dave, seemingly living life backwards, returned to university to study law.

CHAPTER EIGHT
Best-ofs, Clint Eastwood, and the Side Projects (2000-02)

With another Wembley Arena concert wrapped, Blur were officially on hiatus from 16th December 1999, until further notice, emerging only very briefly to play a one-off gig in July 2000 at that year's Meltdown Festival. Held annually on London's Southbank, Meltdown is curated each year by a different act and encompasses music, theatre and visual arts.

They had not intended to play together in 2000, but the offer from that year's curator Scott Walker was too good to turn down. Headlining on Saturday 2nd July (Radiohead headlined the night before), Blur delivered a *13* heavy set that also delved into their back catalogue, featuring album tracks like Blue Jeans (*Modern Life is Rubbish*), Country Sad Ballad Man and Look Inside America (*Blur*), with one of the highlights being To The End, which the band dedicated to Scott Walker, saying. "He had an enormous influence on all our [Blur's] lives."[xxxv]

And then they were gone back to their lives, and away from each other. Dave to his studies, Alex to his cheeses, Graham to tour his new solo album, and Damon into the studio to create the project that would become much bigger on a global scale than anything Blur would ever do, the animated world-music hybrid project, Gorillaz.

There was no announcement made that this was the end of the Blur, the audience knew that there would be more, but what a complicated route it would prove itself to be. The time was certainly right to reset, and that cause was helped along with the first of their best-ofs, which was supported by a new single, Music is My Radar.

Single 22:

Music is My Radar
Released: 16th October 2000; UK Chart Position: 10; Label: Food; Album: *Blur: The Best of*
B-sides: CD1: Black Box; Headist/Into Another (live)
CD2: 7 Days (live); She's So High (live)
Producer: Ben Hillier

UK Official Singles Chart – Top 10 – 22nd October 2000:

1. Stomp – Steps
2. Who Let the Dogs Out – Baha Men
3. Beautiful Day – U2
4. Kids – Robbie Williams/Kylie Minogue
5. Body II Body – Samantha Mumba
6. Silence – Delerium ft. Sarah McClachlan
7. Black Coffee – All Saints
8. Body Groove – Architechs ft. Nana
9. Sunset (Bird of Prey) – Fatboy Slim
10. **Music is My Radar – Blur**

Best-of Album no. 1:

Blur: The Best of
Released: 30th October 2000; UK Chart Position: 3; Label: Food
Track Listing: Beetlebum; Song 2; There's No Other Way; The Universal; Coffee & TV; Parklife; End of the Century; No Distance Left to Run; Tender; Girls & Boys; Charmless Man; She's So High; Country House; To the End; On Your Own; This is a Low; For Tomorrow; Music is My Radar
Producers: Stephen Street, William Orbit, Steve Lovell, Steve Power, Ben Hillier

Trading once again on those art-school roots, which were never that far away from them, the cover of *Blur: The Best of*, featured the four members of the group drawn by the pop-artist and YBA Julian Opie. Another alumnus from Goldsmiths, Opie was more known for his sculpture, and from the eighties onwards, his large scale, overly simplified metal figures were often seen reclining around the urban centres of the country. With the Blur painting he expanded his design to include colour, and each of the members has their own distinct style: Alex's floppy fringe, Graham and Dave's glasses, and Damon's head stuck suggestively at an angle, whilst their eyes remain Opie's trademark black dots.

Like all good best-ofs, the album helped remind people just quite how many great songs Blur had. And it worked in tandem with the cover, which was extremely popular, helping, alongside the music, to cement Blur's reputation as established members of the British cultural landscape, national treasures, there to stay. It was hung in the National Portrait Gallery, where it remains to this day.

UK Official Albums Chart – Top 10 – 5th November 2000:

1. *All That You Can't Leave Behind* – U2
2. *The Greatest Hits* – Texas
3. ***Blur: The Best of* – Blur**
4. *Buzz* – Steps
5. *Parachutes* – Coldplay
6. *Saints & Sinners* – All Saints
7. *White Ladder* – David Gray
8. *The Marshall Mathers LP* – Eminem
9. *Born to Do It* – Craig David
10. *The Collection* – Barry White

Heading toward the Christmas market, it is something of a surprise to see the top 10 made up of just three best-ofs, how different this was to just two years previously when that number was easily doubled. The new millennium brought with it a tranche of new music, and as Blur slipped into third place with their first best-of, we can see an eclectic albums chart made up predominantly of out and out pop: David Gray, Steps, All Saints (whose single Pure Shores was that year's biggest seller); old timers re-inventing themselves for the umpteenth time: U2; rock newcomers soon to dominate: Coldplay; and a hip-hop artist, already looking to be one of the most successful of all time: Eminem, whose work would arguably define the new decade. Blur were in some good company.

Side Projects – Transcopic

And that was it, the last releases from Blur until *Think Tank* in May 2003. Two and a half years away. So, what did everyone get up to next? Well, we already know that Alex and Dave moved away from music, instead focusing on developing other talents. Whilst Graham immersed himself in his solo work. Having released his first solo effort *The Sky is Too High* in August 1998, he went on to release *The Golden D* in June 2000, *Crow Sit on Blood Tree* in August 2001, and *The Kiss of the Morning* in October 2002, during Blur's hiatus, and all on his own indie label based out of Camden, Transcopic.

The roots of Graham's solo career can be traced back to the inclusion of You're So Great on *Blur*, back in 1997. The song, heavily influenced by Pavement, is a lo-fi gem. Coxon bashes out chords on an old acoustic guitar that sounds as if it's been borrowed from the Stanway Comp music portacabin, and which is stuck right on the front of the record, much higher in the mix than would be expected. In the background are added hisses as if the song has been recorded badly (or is being played back on an ancient gramophone), and a distorted vocal that sits at the back of the mix so the listener has to strain to make out the lyrics. The track would come to perfectly iterate Graham's style with his solo work, as well as the other artists who would release music on his label.

Other Transcopic acts included The Buff Medways, Ooberman, and Mower, who were fronted by Coxon's little pet protégé Matt Motte. The first release was the limited edition 7" Noise Vision 80 by noise-vision-smiths Assembly Line People Program in 1998 (produced by Coxon), but it wasn't until *The Sky is Too High* came out in August that year (the label's fifth official release) did it start to gain much traction.

Coxon used his celebrity (and money) as a launch pad to showcase the music of lo-fi indie groups who were not likely to find much of an audience outside of Camden. *The Sky is Too High* picks up from where You're So Great left off, the obviousness of the record scratches and studio noises swapped for roughly hewn acoustic and distorted guitars, the predominant use of the crash and splash symbols, and Coxon's mournful vocal lines. In many ways the album has the feel of being comprised of tracks left over from *Blur*, which to all intents and purposes, it is, but it is also much more than that, finally giving a public voice to the type of music that Coxon and many of his Camden-based followers had been championing for years.

The Sky is Too High found its way to number 31 in the UK Official Albums Chart, its existence marking an important step forward not just for Coxon, but for the rest of Blur too. It gave the erstwhile guitarist an outlet away from the unavoidable cheesiness of *The Great Escape* era Blur, as well as giving its writer the confidence to develop material brought to the group. And not just music, but his artwork as well. Having done the same for *The Sky is Too High,* Graham also painted the cover art for *13*, an impressionistic painting of a topless Alex James.

When Graham was asked to leave Blur during the recording of *Think Tank*, many others in his position may have disappeared into obscurity and waited for the band to reform once they all needed the money. Coxon's next solo album was his most accessible and by far his most successful. *Happiness in Magazines* came out in May 2004 once Blur had split properly and went some way to fill the Blur shaped hole in the UK charts. The album, produced by the band's old friend Stephen Street, reached number 19 in the UK charts and was certified Gold.

Bittersweet Bundle of Misery and Spectacular were strong singles, but it was with the album's first single and key track, the pop-punk anthem Freakin' Out, released in March 2004 (and re-released due to popular demand in October 2004 where it peaked at number 19), that Coxon cemented his career both as a songwriter capable of penning fast-paced indie-pop-punk tunes every bit as good as his former band mate, and that this type of music was still very current. With the track Coxon read the times well and managed to remain honourable to the type of music that he liked to create, as well as fitting alongside Franz Ferdinand and The Kaiser Chiefs and the bands that came in their wake. The success of the album proved to Coxon that he could do it alone, which suitably enough also managed to strengthen his case for being a venerable member of his old group as well, proving that Blur was not just Damon Albarn's vehicle.

Ever the champion of the dispossessed, Coxon's links with the indie world deepened when he played on Pete Doherty's debut solo album in 2009. Doherty, one half of the song writing team and frontmen of early noughties indie legends The Libertines, became just, if not more famous for his drug-taking and general degradation, as he was for his song writing. But what Graham thought was being overlooked by the tabloid stories of drug-fuelled debauchery was his shear talent as a musical artist. Not unfamiliar with this story in his own life, alongside his guitar playing expertise, Graham also offered Doherty the benefit of the reputation he had worked so hard to reclaim since becoming sober himself. The result, *Grace/Wastelands*, is an excellent album full of melodic indie-pop-songs, and its release helped steer Doherty back into the waiting arms of The Libertines, who reformed in 2010.

Coxon has so far released eight solo albums, as well as near single-handedly supporting a whole lo-fi sub-genre of North London bands. In more recent years he has moved into film scoring, just like this contemporaries Thom Yorke and Jonny Greenwood from Radiohead, and he now spends the majority of his time in LA – a far cry from Camden – composing for the Netflix series *The End of the F**king World.*

Side Projects – Gorillaz

Damon Albarn's career went from strength to continued strength during the Blur hiatus (and well beyond it). This was mostly due to the phenomenal success of Gorillaz, but also due to his many other side projects, which included his super-group with Clash bassist Tim Simonon: The Good, The Bad and the Queen; his super-group with Red Hot Chilli Peppers bassist Flea: Rocky Juice and the Moon; his electronic opera *Monkey: Journey to the West* (2008); and scores for stage productions *Dr Dee* (2012) and *Wonder.land* (2016).

But it is Gorillaz, the totally animated act dreamed up when Damon was reeling from his breakup with Justine, and put into existence during Blur's hiatus, that has had the longest lasting impact on music. In 2020 it is almost laughable to call Gorillaz a side project, such is the extent of its success, but that is exactly how the project began life. After a late night drunken conversation in 1998 between a newly single Damon Albarn looking at ways of occupying his time, and his new flat mate and old friend, the cartoonist Jamie Hewlett. Hewlett commented on the state of contemporary music videos on MTV (how if watched for long enough you began to feel like you were in hell), and thus the pair decided to create the world's first virtual group.

Initially, the division of labour was succinct, with Hewlett exclusively handling the visual and Albarn the audio, but it quickly became apparent that the group was about much more than simply the songs and the cartoon images. Although both of those quantities are among some of the most cutting edge in the world. The group's eponymous debut album sold 7 million copies around the world, more than double the biggest selling Blur album, 900,000 in the UK alone; whilst the second album *Demon Days* eclipsed even this in 2005, shifting 1.8 million copies in the UK, and 8 million around the world, 2.4 million copies in the US.

Gorillaz have won one Grammy Award, two MTV Video Music Awards, an NME Award and three MTV Europe Music Awards[xxxvi], as well as the Brit Award for Best British Group in 2018, all this despite the fact they don't even exist.

The virtual element aside, the project is in reality a loose and wide-reaching collective of exalted musicians, singers, rappers and producers, with Albarn in the lead. The project allows him the opportunity of travelling the world and playing with some of the most influential – and often, most left-field – musicians of all time. From the band's third album *Plastic Beach* in 2010 for example, the guests included Snoop Dogg, Lou Reed, Mos Def, Bobby Womack, Gruff Rhys (Super Furry Animals), Mark E. Smith (The Fall), Mick Jones and Paul Simonon (The Clash), Kano, Bashy, De La Soul, Little Dragon, Hypnotic Brass Ensemble, sinfonia ViVA, and the Lebanese National Orchestra for Oriental Arabic Music.[xxxvii] Many of whom you would never imagine appearing with Blur. The project therefore stretches some of Albarn's musical muscles that Blur just doesn't quite manage to reach.

The idea of a cartoon band originally provided something of a quirky excuse for Albarn to release material not deemed right for Blur, or under a solo-project heading, notably dance music, electronica and hip hop, music developed traditionally from Afro-Caribbean origins, that people might not immediately identify with an indie-pop star like Damon; but it soon became something much more substantial, both musically and perhaps more importantly, visually, with cutting edge graphics soon becoming the norm for the virtual group.

The first album was recorded in 2000, with the first music arriving in the form of the EP, Tomorrow Comes Today, in November 2000. Having four tracks, the EP was ineligible for the charts, so it wasn't until Clint Eastwood was picked up by commercial radio in March 2001, reaching number 4, and the album reaching number 3 in April 2001, that Albarn and Hewitt were given the first clue of how well the new act would chime with the record buying public.

Success bred success, and there was a marked visual development between the group's first and second album, the advancement in the visual image between the video for Clint Eastwood and Feel Good Inc. as notably stark as the jump from black and white to colour film, and the band's visual element has only developed since.

This is not to downplay the quality of music on the first album though. As is to be expected of Albarn, the songs are cleverly constructed, with each composition its own intricately layered symphony, influenced – despite the noted change in musical direction – by the work that Albarn had produced up to this point. Take lead single Clint Eastwood for example, behind that distinctive Dan the Automator beat and rap by Del the Funky Homosapien, lies a melodica line – a keyboard come trumpet like instrument with a haunting quality that would be used frequently enough by Albarn on the Gorillaz records to become a notifiable motif of the group's – that soon begins to echo the circus carnival music box reminiscent of *Blur*, thus drawing the influence of the Southern Gothic and all its associations to this ramshackle collective of outsiders.

The Southern Gothic influence on the visual element of the group is apt, the whole idea of the characters plays on the uncanny, the fear of the other, their appearance reminding of an eclectic group of travelling carnival folk that is distinctly synonymous with the genre. Drummer Russell is the silent strong man, juxtaposed neatly against guitarist Noodle, the tiny yet mysterious exotic foreigner. Bassist Murdoc is the strange one, the magician or alchemist, unpredictable yet enticing, and the excellently named lead singer 2-D (his name adapted from Massive Attack's leader Robert "3D" Del Naja, and the fact that he is a two-dimensional figure) is the ring master and Albarn's alter ego. Amongst the many stories that have been created for the group over the years, the audience is invited to ask how on earth such a disparate group met in the first instance? And if they aren't human, just what exactly are they?

If the Southern Gothic is central to the band's image, then it is equally influenced by Japanese Manga, clearly a large part Hewlett drew on in developing his style. Take the flying windmill from the ever more sophisticated video for first single from second album and number 2 hit in the UK, Feel Good Inc., and its direct homage to *Howl's Moving Castle*, the classic Studio Ghibli animated film by Hayao Miyazaki from 2004, a year before the single's release.

The group's creators wear their influences in plain sight – just as The Rolling Stones did with American blues – and it therefore becomes clear that both image and sound meld together the perception of a group that draws on classic tropes to create something altogether fantastic.

As the band's time together has continued, Albarn and Hewlett have revelled in creating intricate back stories for each of the group's four members, particularly since the band had a break in 2012 when Albarn and Hewitt had a real life falling out, and it looked unlikely there would be any new material. They reconvened in 2014 and to date the group has released six studio albums, as well as two B-sides albums and a greatest hits singles collection. The long awaited Gorillaz film is still apparently in gestation, the anticipation now quite mammoth.

With Gorillaz and his many other side projects it is difficult to underestimate the importance of the position that Damon Albarn has carved out for himself in the last twenty years, carefully but not wilfully placing himself as the modern renaissance man, popping up with a new project every five minutes, his desire and drive to try new musical projects seemingly limitless. He even found time to collaborate with the man who had once upon a time wished for him to die of AIDS. Noel Gallagher guested on the 2017 Gorillaz track We Got the Power, from the band's fifth album *Humanz*, and the two are now firm friends, much to the British press' displeasure.

CHAPTER NINE
Think Tank and Fallen Heroes (2002-04)

By the time Blur reconvened to record what would become their seventh album *Think Tank* in November 2001, there was no longer any hiding the huge cracks that had been long papered over. They had been on hiatus for nearly two years, and the hope that the break would have fixed them faded almost immediately when recording began. Graham, his drinking now much publicised in the music press, decided to do something about it and booked himself into the Priory, London's celeb spotted drug and alcohol rehabilitation centre, for a month. By the time he emerged Blur were well into the recording sessions and he was told in no uncertain terms that his services would no longer be required. Damon, choosing to call Graham's bluff after years of bad behaviour, never really displayed much penchant for guitar before, but went on to play all of the guitar parts on the album. A move which at the time was taken for total megalomania by Coxon.

This may have seemed like an overly harsh move from his band mates, but it is important to remember the events that led up to this most difficult decision. As previously stated, *13* had been recorded amidst an environment where bad behaviour (not just on Coxon's behalf) had been condoned, and so once the accompanying tour had been completed and work on the album and the subsequent singles tour had run their promotional life span, the decision was made to take the time off. So for him to be nowhere to be seen when they were due to get back together, one could see how it may have looked to the rest of the band.

In retrospect, with the ability of being able to look back at events from the perspective of the band making friends again, Coxon's departure seems like it took on more of a symbolic nature than it may have appeared at the time. Basically, something needed to give, after all those years with the four of them getting on each other's nerves, something was going to snap eventually. And once it happened and the penance was paid, all the members were able to make up and move on. Alex James had said some derogatory things about Gorillaz in the press that needed fixing with Damon once the band were back in the studio, meaning that tensions were already fraught. Graham's drinking just provided the catalyst that sparked the flame. But, once the boil was popped and the pressure was released, they were ready to start again. Still, seeing Blur play live in 2003 was something of a subdued affair, Coxon's sub Simon Tong (formerly of The Verve) careful to skulk near the back of the stage so as not to infuriate Coxon fans any further than necessary.

Single 23:

Out of Time
Released: 14th April 2003; UK Chart Position: 5; Label: Parlophone; Album: *Think Tank*
B-sides: Money Makes Me Crazy (Marrakech mix)
Producer: Ben Hillier

UK Official Singles Chart – Top 10 – 20th April 2003:

1. Make Luv – Room 5 ft. Oliver Cheatham
2. American Life – Madonna
3. In Da Club – 50 Cent
4. Come Undone – Robbie Williams
5. **Out of Time – Blur**
6. Move your Feet – Junior Senior
7. Cry – Kym Marsh
8. Spirit in the Sky – Gareth Gates ft. the Kumars

9. Speechless – D-Side
10. All I Have – Jennifer Lopez ft. LL Cool J

Although Damon had been keeping his finger on the pulse with Gorillaz, chart music hadn't changed a huge amount since Blur's last single. The likes of Madonna, Jennifer Lopez and Robbie Williams were still present in the top 10, the only major addition being that the Simon Cowell led reality TV stars were starting to infiltrate. Here represented by Gareth Gates, runner-up on the first series of *Pop Idol* in 2001. Ever since *Popstars* first aired in December 2000, all and sundry had been clamouring to find the short cut to fame that a reality TV show offered the great and the hopeful. *Pop Idol* changed the format in October 2001, when it placed the contest in front of an audience, and more votes were cast that saw Will Young crowned the first winner, than in that year's UK general election.

By 2002, the charts were finding themselves saturated with reality stars. The first series of X-Factor, where groups, plus male and female singers competed against one another, was launched in 2004 and the Christmas number 1s were booked in for the next five years. Interestingly, X-Factor never took off in America, which much preferred the simplicity of the *Pop Idol* format, in which one singer was pitted against another.

The public finally began to hit back against the total dominance of the Christmas number 1 slot, when a Facebook campaign took Rage Against the Machine's Killing in the Name of to number 1 in 2009, one place ahead of that year's X-Factor winner Joe McElderry. Simon Cowell called the campaign bullying…how ironic.

Album 7:

Think Tank
Released: 5th May 2003; UK Chart Position: 1; Label: Parlophone
Track Listing: Ambulance; Out of Time; Crazy Beat; Good Song; On the Way to the Club; Brothers and Sisters; Caravan; We've Got a File on You; Moroccan Peoples Revolutionary Bowls Club; Sweet Song; Jets; Gene by Gene; Battery in the Leg; bonus track – Me, White Noise (ft. Phil Daniels)
Producers: Ben Hillier; Norman Cook (Crazy Beat; Gene by Gene); William Orbit

UK Official Albums Chart – Top 10 – 11th May 2003:

1. ***Think Tank* – Blur**
2. *Justified* – Justine Timberlake
3. *Elephant* – White Stripes
4. *Busted* – Busted
5. *American Life* – Madonna
6. *Stripped* – Christina Aguilera
7. *Come Away With Me* – Norah Jones
8. *Let Go* – Avril Lavigne
9. *A Rush of Blood to the Head* – Coldplay
10. *Say you Will* – Fleetwood Mac

Think Tank was Blur's fifth consecutive album to reach number 1 in the albums chart, which was no real surprise considering the band's position of standing and reputation by this point in their career. With the second wave of Britpop – that would see guitar bands such as Razorlight, The Libertines, Pigeon Detectives, Elbow, Kaiser Chiefs and of course Arctic Monkeys, dominate the charts once more – still a year or so off, pop music appeared to be experiencing something of a coming-of-age moment. Both Justine Timberlake and Christina Aguilera released grown-up R'n'B flavoured pop records, whilst the biggest record of the year came from Norah Jones and her debut album *Come Away With Me*, a smooth jazz-lite album directly lifting influence by the likes of Billie Holiday, Ella Fitzgerald and Nina Simone. Teenagers were listening to records that their parents would have bought, for the first time since the fifties.

There was little doubt who Britain's biggest band were by this point though. Coldplay were only on their second album in 2003, *A Rush of Blood to the Head*, released nearly a year earlier, but they were undisputed worldwide superstars, having taken the more melancholic aspects of Oasis and Blur, and made mournful ballads with echo-drenched guitar lines popular once more. Music it seemed, was on its way back to the middle classes once more.

Think Tank

Given the circumstances of its creation, *Think Tank* is a surprisingly solid album. Much lower key than its two predecessors, the band decided not to go big in the era of Frank Ferdinand, The Libertines and The Darkness, but were content to take a more reclined seat at the elder statesmen table. The album is at its best when it taps into the gentle stream of sombre meditation that flows through it. Singles Out of Time and Good Song, both tinged with a gentle melancholia, set the tone for the album, portraying a more introspective yet markedly confident side to Albarn's song writing. Sweet Song is just that, a beautiful little sweet song that would probably have been kept for a B-side in another lifetime, but here helps to steer the album toward the gentle tone that dictates.

There is little doubt that this is Damon's album. The remaining band members happy to find themselves in the back seat of the car, the passenger seat left empty for this outing. Coxon appears only on Battery in the Leg, the final song on the album, his haunting chromatic scales ascending and then descending between verses, drifting across the song like a ghost at the feast. Cleverly, Albarn never tries to replace Coxon or replicate his playing, rather he works around the lack of lead guitar by layering keyboard lines and those all too familiar bleeps and whirls from *13*. There is even a jazz sax solo tagged on the end of Jets to help liven things up.

You might expect more keyboard parts, but Damon is all too aware that this is a Blur album, and not a Gorillaz one. He plays guitar on every track, but limits his playing to the gentle picked arpeggios of Out of Time (complemented by a simple acoustic guitar solo that he also played live), or the simple rock riffs of Jets and Gene by Gene. The latter track is one of two produced by Fatboy Slim himself, Norman Cook, bought in, alongside *13* producer William Orbit, to help augment the sound beyond its straightforward rock roots.

Buried in what feels like an improvised jam that goes nowhere, the chorus to Cook track Gene by Gene comes from nowhere, and is pure Damon Albarn, just as the chorus to On the Way to the Club does the same thing, leaping out at the listener, fooled by a substandard verse melody. And this is where *Think Tank* finds its strength. Damon's ear for a good melody. Now so well practised after 12 years writing hits, that he can seemingly pick a good song (pun intended) from anywhere.

Rather it is with the other Cook track Crazy Beat, also the album's second single, that the album begins to fall down. Beginning with a cringe inducing ploppy sampled sound, Blur are far too old for this type of song, and probably were back when they were making *Leisure*. We've Got a File on You falls into the same camp, its jabby Coxon-esque punk chords are at least mercifully brief, and the listener is left thinking the album would be much better if they had stuck to the gentle melancholia of Out of Time and Good Song.

Damon later called *Think Tank* his protest album, many of the songs written as a direct result of Tony Blair's unlawful invasion of Iraq in May 2003, but if he was trying to offer the album credence by drenching it in this unnecessary moniker then he probably shouldn't have bothered. Damon, and what was left of Blur, had proved themselves perfectly capable of writing and recording a decent album, and at this point, that really should have been enough. They just should have left Crazy Beat on the cutting room floor.

The key theme that comes across on the record is of love and domestic happiness, "I just wanna be, darling, with you," sings Damon on On Our Way to the Club, and, "you seem very beautiful to me," he adds on Good Song. After the heart wrenching breakdown of his relationship with Justine, and subsequent pouring out of his soul onto *13*, *Think Tank* is a marked juxtaposition, reflecting Damon's relative domestic contentedness. He married Suzi Winstanley not long after splitting with Justine, and he became a father in 1999, Missy being 5 when *Think Tank* came out.

The album was recorded mostly at 13, Damon's London studio, but they also made a big thing at the time of moving briefly to Morocco to lay down some of the tracks, refitting a barn in Marakesh. Damon claimed to have written most of the lyrics for the album whilst there, including the song Put it Back Together, which he gifted to Cook, who included it on his fourth album *Palookaville* in 2004; but the space the North African country gave him seems to provide him with the opportunity of reflection, rather than any direct influence.

In Morocco for just a month, the band completed Crazy Beat, Gene by Gene and quite predictably Moroccan Peoples Revolutionary Bowls Club. If fans had expected an African influences on the album, they were to be disappointed, but Damon was clearly influenced by the world he saw around him, and African influences popped up on much of his later solo work, including Gorillaz's tracks.

Single 24:

Crazy Beat
Released: 7th July 2003; UK Chart Position: 18; Label: Parlophone; Album: *Think Tank*
B-sides: Don't Be; Crazy Beat (video)
Producer: Norman Cook

UK Official Singles Chart – Top 10 – 13th July 2003:

1. Crazy in Love – Beyonce
2. Hollywood – Madonna
3. Feel Good Time – Pink ft. William Orbit
4. Real Things – Javine
5. Bring me to Life – Evanescence
6. Business – Eminem
7. No Letting Go – Wayne Wonder
8. Fast Food Song – Fast Food Rockers
9. Ignition Remix – R Kelly
10. Come on Over – Kym Marsh

……………………..

18. Crazy Beat – Blur

Blur's lowest charting single since 1994, Crazy Beat was released as a counterpoint to Out of Time, and what would be the band's last single before their split, Good Song. The track was poppy enough, but if the idea was to try and connect with the band's punky roots, it felt at odds with the grown-up sound that comes across so fluently on *Think Tank*. It says much about Blur's enduring popularity that it reached the top 20 at all.

At number 1 that week was another 'crazy' song, this time Crazy in Love, the part original/part mashup R'n'B classic from the one-woman music industry, Beyonce Knowles. Blur's old friend William Orbit was also now making himself known as part of what would become a very prolific period with the first of his collaborations, this time with Pink, who was also in the process of delivering what would be an incredible run of successful singles and albums, Feel Good Time was her eighth top 10 UK single. It certainly seemed that rock music was the furthest thing from everyone's minds in 2003.

Single 25:

Good Song
Released: 6th October 2003; UK Chart Position: 22;
Label: Parlophone; Album: *Think Tank*
B-sides: CD: Me, White Noise (alternate version)
7": Morricone
Producer: Ben Hillier

UK Official Singles Chart – Top 10 – 12th October 2003:

1. Where is the Love – Black Eyed Peas
2. Baby Boy – Beyonce ft. Sean Paul
3. Superstar – Jamelia
4. Sweet Dreams my LA Ex – Rachel Stevens
5. I Believe in a Thing Called Love – The Darkness
6. White Flag – Dido
7. 12:51 – The Strokes
8. Sundown – S Club 8
9. Carnival Girl – Texas Kardinal Offishall

10. Say Cheese (Smile Please) – Fast Food Rockers

……………………

22. Good Song – Blur

Charting outside the top 20 for the first time since the singles from *Modern Life is Rubbish* back in 1993, Good Song was a classic Blur releases despite the seemingly poor charting performance. Its gentle strum carries a message of happiness in domesticity via a beautiful, gentle melody. And considering the pomposity of that week's number 1, the Black Eyed Peas huge single Where is the Love, itself a clear nod to seventies Marvin Gaye, it is easy to see how Good Song may have become lost.

The Darkness were at number 5 with their biggest hit I Believe in a Thing Called Love, signalling a surge for British rock was just around the corner, and just two months away, the mega-hit Take Me Out by Scottish dance-rockers Franz Ferdinand would help kickstart the second wave of Britpop. But it was the Kaiser Chiefs that would pick up where Blur left off. Their tales of everyday life lived as an outsider, set against fiery indie-rock, fitted in perfectly with the likes of Pulp and Blur. They even called their debut album *Employment*, a nod of sorts to Blur's first album *Leisure*, and Damon would later hand over the baton of British rock music to singer Ricky Wilson in a bar in 2005, by holding out his hands as a bridge for Wilson to pass under.

After the release of Good Song, there was just the small matter of the epic 84 date *Think Tank* tour, that took the band all over the world once more, from Japan to North America to Europe, ending with a run of UK dates that culminated at the Bournemouth International Centre on 12th December 2003. And then it was all over, no more live concerts for six years, or new music for nine. The band members each returning to their own lives once more.

Damon had always made it clear that Blur was about more than any individual members, and *Think Tank* made that starkly clear. Alex James and Dave Rowntree relied on the income Blur generated, whilst with the success of Gorillaz, Damon no longer did. *Think Tank* needed to be made for financial reasons, and Damon committed to that, hence why he felt so betrayed when Graham didn't show up. The band needed to continue, even if one of its defining features was missing.

Despite being thrown out of the band, Graham proved himself contented releasing his own records on his own label, but in truth there was no Blur without him, and it seemed sensible to everyone when the band quietly laid down their instruments once the *Think Tank* tour was completed, and went their own separate ways. Again, with hindsight, this all seems like poetic justice, the band needed to split so that they could come back together much stronger years later, but in 2003, just like *Faulty Towers*, which was finished after just 12 episodes, there was the feeling that the story had not yet resolved.

Damon went back to his many solo projects, whilst Rowntree was soon practising law for a Liverpool Street firm of solicitors, eventually running (unsuccessfully) for the Camden Labour party seat for Parliament. His dreams of running for office were finally realised when he was elected as a county councillor in the Norfolk County Council elections in 2017.

In between his regular columns for Q magazine, and monthly articles on farming for the Sunday broadsheets, Alex James found the time to write and release his memoirs, the excellently named *Bit of a Blur*, in 2007. The book was quickly ear-marked as one of the definitive recollections of the Britpop period – still of such fascination to people ten years on – and had no small hand in reuniting Coxon with the other band members, due to James' favourable description of his old friend, and his key role within the band. As 2007 tipped over into 2008, the feeling began to spread through the camp that that perhaps there was a way forward for the group, and in the end, it seemed that all it took was an Eccles cake.

CHAPTER TEN
Tomorrow Comes Today – Reformation, *Parklive* and *The Magic Whip* (2007-20)

Big of a Blur

In his book, Alex James manages to tell the band's story from the point of view of rose-tinted nostalgia, whilst remaining aware of his own, and his band mates' many short comings, therefore shaping fully rounded, very readable characters. We know the story well but have to keep reading to find out what happens next. Knowing his audience, James jumps right to the juicy stuff, and the band is formed in the first chapter, the reader immediately shown a picture of just how close the four of them were in the early days: "We both wanted to be in the best band ever shaped on earth, but all boys with guitars do."[xxxviii]

As the story develops though, James' story begins to diverge from that of the band, and he soon discovers new interests, notably astronomy, cheese and most importantly, the Groucho Club. The narrative manages to avoid being deplored as a naming-dropping cash-in, because of James' clear enjoyment in re-telling the stories all these years later, and his shear audacity in having lived such a life. Amongst his many famous friends, the two notable stands outs are the actor Keith Allen and the leader of the YBAs, Damien Hirst, of whom James' says: "He was an irresistible combination of rudeness and wit…he was obviously a genius."[xxxix].

Where you might expect a Damon Albarn autobiography to be packed with anecdotes about creating music in various different guises, as James' story develops, the music slips further into the background, until it becomes just his day job, so monotonous to be uncommentable, like working in an office or a factory (neither of which he has ever done). His band mates feature less and less as he heads down the rabbit hole of hedonism: "I stopped having sex occasionally, but only so that I could have more drugs."[xl] In just the same way that another famous bass player, New Order's Peter Hook (a good friend of James'), does a similar thing in his autobiography *Substance*. By the time of New Order's biggest success, around 1990, the members could no longer be in the same backstage area as each other.

Band mates outgrow each other, and in order to remain together to make music, they have to socialise separately. No surprises there, but unlike Hook's story, James' book managed to remind the members of Blur just what it was that they had together, and what they could possibly have again. And then all it took was a phone call. The four members of the band had been together after Graham's departure, at Alex's wedding in 2003, where various hatchets were buried, but by 2008 Damon and Graham had met up, bonding over a shared Eccles cake, eaten on the doorstep of a North London flat, discussing the possibility of playing together again.

Things began slowly, with the band booked in to headline the Saturday night at Glastonbury on 27th June 2009, they started with a handful of warm up dates, including the East Anglian Railway Museum in Colchester, the site of their very first gig back in 1988. The band's second best-of was released the same day that they played the Rough Trade store on Brick Lane in East London, helping to remind people of exactly who this band were.

Best-of Album no. 2:

Midlife: A Beginner's Guide to Blur
Released: 15th June 2009; UK Chart Position: 20; Label: Parlophone
Track Listing: CD1: Beetlebum; Girls & Boys; For Tomorrow (extended version); Coffee & TV; Out of

Time; Blue Jeans; Song 2; Bugman; He Thought of Cars; Death of a Party; The Universal; Sing; This is a Low
CD2: Tender; She's So High; Chemical; Good Song; Parklife; Advert; Popscene; Stereotypes; Trimm Trabb; Badhead; Strange News from Another Star; Battery in Your Leg
Producers: Stephen Street, William Orbit, Ben Hillier, Steve Lovell, Steve Power

UK Official Albums Chart – Top 10 – 21st June 2009:

1. *West Ryder Pauper Lunatic Asylum* – Kasabian
2. *Sunny Side Up* – Paolo Nutini
3. *Greatest Hits* – Bruce Springsteen and the E Street Band
4. *Let it Roll* – George Harrison
5. *Love & War* – Daniel Merriweather
6. *Only by the Night* – Kings of Leon
7. *The Very Best of* – Jim Reeves
8. *The End* – Black Eyed Peas
9. *Lines Vines and Trying Times* – Jonas Brothers
10. *Hits Out of Hell* – Meatloaf

…………………………………………………

20. *Midlife: A Beginner's Guide to Blur* – Blur

By 2009 physical record sales were at an all time low, but with streaming not counted toward chart positioning until 2014, they were still the only way to gauge what people were listening to. Despite Blur's best-of slipping in at a not remarkable number 20, rock music did seem to be back in favour, Oasis' heirs Kasabian at the top spot, with their third album and second number 1, and even former Beatle George Harrison finding his way to number 4 with a new best-of (despite having been dead since 2002). The biggest band at the time though were Kings of Leon, whose fourth album, the mega hit *Only by the Night*, was still at number 6 after 39 weeks on the chart.

Where their first best-of had featured just their singles (aside from This is a Low, a live favourite) *Midlife* included various album tracks, from across their career, hindsight through the intervening years affording them the opportunity of being able to see which songs had lasted. Sing, for example, popularised by Danny Boyle in *Trainspotting* back in 1996, is featured, as is the politically charged Death of a Party, as well as the material from *Think Tank*, not originally included on their first best-of.

Live Albums 1&2:

All the People: Blur Live at Hyde Park 02/07/09 & 03/07/09
Released: 23rd August 2009; UK Chart Positions: 02/07 – 70; 03/07 – 44; Label: Parlophone
Track Listing: CD1: She's So High; Girls & Boys; Tracy Jacks; There's Not Other Way; Jubilee; Badhead; Beetlebum; Out of Time; Trimm Trabb; Coffee & TV; Tender
CD2: Country House; Oily Water; Chemical World; Sunday Sunday; Parklife; End of the Century; To The End; This is a Low; Popscene; Advert; Song 2; Death of a Party; For Tomorrow; The Universal

UK Official Albums Chart – Top 10 – 30th August 2009:

1. *Humbug* – Arctic Monkeys
2. *One Love* – David Guetta
3. *Ready for the Weekend* – Calvin Harris
4. *The End* – Black Eyed Peas
5. *Catch 22* – Tinchy Stryder
6. *Sunny Side Up* – Paolo Nutini

7. *I Am Sasha Fierce* – Beyonce
8. *The Essential* – Michael Jackson
9. *Songs for the Truths for Me* – James Morrison
10. *Lungs* – Florence & The Machines

....

44. ***All the People: Blur Live at Hyde Park 03/07/09*** **– Blur**

70. ***All the People: Blur Live at Hyde Park 02/07/09*** **– Blur**

And then came the live albums. From the opening chords of She's So High, via a heated Girls & Boys, through Tracy Jacks and There's No Other Way and Jubilee, the first night at Hyde Park is like the band have never been away. The crowd were immediately on side, and it was not just oldies there the first time around, like your author, but many youngsters made up the front row of the concert, cheering along to every word from every track like they were born to it. Damon's voice is slightly more growly, but otherwise this could be 1999 all over again. After the run of warm up gigs, and the triumphant outdoor Glastonbury performance, the band are on the best form they could be and are clearly loving it. Hyde Park provided the backdrop to the characters and the world of *Parklife*, and this is the perfect homecoming concert.

Although they would eventually record a new album in 2015, Blur's return was all about the live gig, where they managed to connect with their massive audience one-to-one, and this double album –quadruple album if you count the fact sets from both nights were released – was released as a way of marking the occasion, rather than intended for any real commercial value. Particularly because their two best-ofs had done just that by this point. Blur reformed for themselves and for each other, Damon's phenomenal success with Gorillaz totally separated away from the cultural importance that Blur provided to the times, and for the people. Gorillaz may have outsold anything Blur ever did – Alex James' side project Fat Les' single Vindaloo outsold any single Blur released – but to focus on that would be to miss the point.

After Hyde Park the band took the newly revamped outfit on the road proper, playing the excellently named Théâtre Antique in Lyon, France, T in the Park in Scotland, and Oxygen in Ireland, before calling it day once more. Their comeback had been assured, and not only did this reinvigorate their own career, it also laid the pathway for a string of bands reforming over the coming years. Most notably Sleeper, the Bluetones, Supergrass, Pulp, Shed 7, Menswear, Dodgy, Space, bands that are still performing today, and for whom the renewed interest in Britpop, spearheaded by the likes of the *Starshaped* club night, has meant a whole second phase of their career.

But just like Britpop, Blur did it first and did it best, signalling both the importance and brilliance of their music, and its enduring quality not only with their existing audience, but with a new audience. The band took another couple of years off, but it didn't feel like it, everyone aware that they could be back at any time. When they did emerge again in 2012, it was the cheery sounds of Ray Winstone (perhaps Phil Daniels wasn't available) and the accolade of being awarded the lifetime achievement award at the 2012 Brit Awards. Before that though, the band's first full length documentary film since *Starshaped* was released in January 2010.

Documentary no. 2

No Distance Left to Run
Released: 19th January 2010
Director: Dylan Southern & Will Lovelace

A big part of getting the band back together was making sure that the process and the experience was documented. Help came in the form of directors Dylan Southern and Will Lovelace, who with just one music video credit for Franz Ferdinand to their names, were an untested paring, but the result is a warm, watchable documentary that puts the band at the centre, allowing them to tell their own story. Interspaced with archive footage taken from, amongst other places, the band's previous documentary *Starshaped*, it shows just how far they had come since 1993.

The film is warts and all as it should be, but there are no shaking black and white camera angles, à la Grant Gee's *Meeting People is Easy* (1998), or the band only shown in arty silhouette, as in Julian Temple's 2000 Sex Pistols' documentary *The Filth and the Fury*. Rather, the band are front and centre, and as eloquent as they have ever been. Alex James, always reliable for a solid one-liner is immediately quotable: "Britpop was 100% Damon Albarn's idea", and Graham Coxon lays his problems with alcohol out on the table, only too happy to talk about his rejection from the band, now that everyone is friends again. It is Damon Albarn who is the biggest surprise though, actively keen to discuss the band's successes and failures in exactly the same way that he was clearly so uncomfortable doing so in *Live Forever* back in 2003, coming across as testy and unapproachable. He even finally admits that it was his idea to move the date of the release of Country House in order to clash with the release of Roll With It, "I thought that's what it was all about".

Released in 2010, the film started something of a trend for long form documentaries about formerly great bands looking to set the record straight, including Shane Meadows' 2012 Stone Roses film, *Made of Stone*, Brett Morgen's 2012 Rolling Stones film *Crossfire Hurricane*, and Mat Whitecross' 2016 Oasis film *Supersonic*. However, where Morgen and Whitecross follow Julien Temple's decisions of reducing the present day band members to just voice-over, and Meadows' film is so immersive, it feels like an episode of *Made in England*, Southern and Lovelace's film is about the band's reunion, and is told resolutely from their point of view. Ultimately it shows a band whose members are comfortable not only in their own skin, but once again, with each other. They are a joy to be around, or spend time with even through a TV screen, and the film helps to showcase what a good idea it was that they got back together when they did.

The Year of the Dragon – 2012

2012 was a big year for the UK, and a big year for Blur. Firstly they joined the exalted ranks of those with a lifetime achievement Brit award, and then that summer the Olympic Games took over London, and the world, gentrifying Stratford in the process. Having been bid for and won by then London mayor Ken Livingstone back in 2005, the games promised to be the event of the millennium so far. Livingstone had history with Blur, having appeared on the rather odd *Great Escape* track Ernold Same back in 1995, five years before he became mayor. The games though were going to be delivered by Livingstone's Conservative counterpart and successor, Boris Johnson, in his pre-Prime Minister guise of London Mayor, if the mayor was played by a character from the *Beano*.

Bojo played the whole event like it was his idea, complete with being caught halfway down a zip-wire in a stunt that made him look like a fool. Johnson is in no way a fool though, despite his continued actions to the contrary, and he understood the importance of the London Olympics in re-establishing London, and the UK by proxy, as a global player.

Before that though, in February, Blur were honoured at that year's Brit Awards. After the minute long video that seemed to consist of footage lifted directly from *No Distance Left to Run*, the band thanked everyone they had ever come across, before running through a set of Girls & Boys, Song 2, Parklife, Tender and This is a Low.

Sadly it was a somewhat muted affair, the days of Liam Gallagher singing "shite-life" long behind the music industry. Only Adele, of all people, caused controversy, when she complained after her acceptance speech for best album was cut short to allow for Blur's award. But then Blur's performance of Tender was cut short too, due to the show overrunning. Where was Liam when we needed him? Brother Noel did perform AKA…What a Life! at the performance though, showing just how far the two bands had come since squabbling on and off stage in 1995 and 1996.

It is of course a total coincidence that Oasis split in 2009, just when Blur were getting back together, but ultimately it had no less important a cultural impact at the time. The two bands, though proving themselves again and again polar opposites apart in terms of background and style, are linked by their intrinsic importance to such a momentous time in British music, which reflected the best the country had to offer as it stood on a world platform.

In 2012, the world platform was back, its eyes once again falling on London because of the Olympics. The cultural aspect of the event, the Cultural Olympiad, curated by Lord Tony Hall, looked to have just as big an impact as the sport. The then Chief Executive of the Royal Opera House (he took on the role of Director-General of the BBC in November 2012) bolstered his team by employing film director Danny Boyle, putting him in charge of the opening and closing night celebrations. Boyle of course, was another artist who had made his name in the mid-nineties during Cool Britannia.

Damon was one of the musicians involved in the festival, which ran between 21st June and 9th September, but Blur's biggest involvement came by them simply being themselves and hosting another huge one-off event in Hyde Park on 12th August. Just as each country offered their greatest sportspeople to participate in the sporting events, so too did the UK and London offer its greatest artists out to the world. Alongside Blur in Hyde Park, their old friend Damien Hirst had a major retrospective at the Tate Modern that summer. Another of Britain's greatest artists Lucien Freud also had his biggest retrospective at the National Portrait Gallery, the Globe Theatre ran a season of some of Shakespeare's greatest plays, including Henry V, and Mark Rylance as Richard III, and the British Film Institute screened every film by one of the greatest film directors of all time, Alfred Hitchcock, including restoring the nine silent movies he made in Britain before heading off to Hollywood.

That summer was like a world's fair for the modern age, every bit as important as the Great Exhibition of 1851. But where Prince Albert's event was designed to showcase Britain's role as an industrial leader, the Olympics drew the world's attention to how far Britain had come since the industrial revolution, and how it now expressed itself through sport and art, multi-culturalism engrained at all levels. The whole thing was a huge success, and had a large impact on shining a positive light on Britain, instilling a sense of earned – positive – patriotism, that people from all walks of life could feel for their country. Ramifications are still being felt today, notably on Britain's current performances in the world of sport, from the cricket world cup winners of 2019, to the football world cup semi-finalists a year earlier. Those playing for their country today had been teenagers or younger during the Olympics, and the access to sports tuition has helped change lives. Hopefully it won't be another 100 years before Britain gets the Olympics again.

As is Britannia's wont though, four years later all that hard work threatened to be undone when the populous voted by 51.89% to leave the European Union.

The vote to leave the EU was a protest vote by the people of Britain, sick with being patronised by a weak government, and an even weaker Prime Minister, who sold his soul to the right of his party in exchange for a majority in the House of Commons. Brexit, and the government's clear lack of understanding on how it should be delivered, has made Britain look like something of an embarrassment on a world stage, in complete disproportion to how well the 2012 Olympics made it look. Luckily for Britannia, what happened later on in 2016 across the Pond, with the other party in the special relationship, made them look even worse.

But back to Blur, who in July 2012 released their first new single for nine years.

Single 26:

Under the Westway/The Puritan
Released: 2nd July 2012; UK Chart Position: 34; Label: Parlophone; Album: n/a
B-sides: n/a
Producer: Blur

UK Official Singles Chart – Top 10 – 8th July 2012:

1. Payphone – Maroon 5 ft. Wiz Khalifa
2. Don't Wake me Up – Chris Brown
3. This is Love – Will I Am ft. Eva Simons
4. Whistle – Flo Rida
5. Black Heart - Stooshie
6. Feel the Love – Rudimental ft. John Newman
7. We Are Young – Fun ft. Janelle Monae
8. Princess of China – Coldplay & Rihanna
9. Wide Awake – Katy Perry

10. Call My Name – Cheryl

…………………………

34. Under the Westway – Blur

The Westway is the A-road that runs through much of West London, and it had previously featured in the lyrics of For Tomorrow, linking the band with their past and the version of Britain that they conjured up in those early years, so placing the song withing the context of a time and a place beyond the now. Under the Westway is Blur of old, but now grown up. More sensible, more considered. It is grand without being epic, not as understated or melancholic as anything from *Think Tank*, or as out there as anything from *13*, just somewhere in the middle, summing up Blur's work neatly.

They didn't really need to release a new single to promote their activity in 2012, it may well have made sense to put it out ahead of *The Magic Whip* in 2015, but again, that would mean they were buying into the traditional route of releasing single and album, rather than just putting out music as and when they felt the need to. The typical time of the band's existence: single, album, tour, repeat, was over for Blur now. They were bigger than that. More culturally important. They didn't need to do this, they wanted to.

Live Album no. 3:

Parklive
Released: iTunes: 13th August 2012, CD: 20th August 2012; UK Chart Positions: 91; Label: Parlophone
Track Listing: CD1: Girls & Boys; London Loves; Tracy Jacks; Jubilee; Beelebum; Coffee & TV; Out of Time; Young and Lovely; Trimm Trabb; Caramel; Sunday Sunday; Country House; Parklife
CD2: Colin Zeal; Popscene; Advert; Song 2; No Distance Left to Run; Tender; This is a Low; Sing;

Under the Westway/Intermission; End of the Century; For Tomorrow; The Universal

UK Official Albums Chart – Top 10 – 19th August 2012:

1. *Our Version of Events* – Emeli Sande
2. *Fall to Grace* – Paloma Faith
3. + – Ed Sheeran
4. *Life in the Beautiful Light* – Amy MacDonald
5. *Overexposed* – Maroon 5
6. *The Seldom Seen Kid* – Elbow
7. *Who You Are* – Jessie J
8. *Talk That Talk* – Rihanna
9. *Ryan O'Shaughnessy* – Ryan O'Shaughnessy
10. *Up All Night* – One Direction

…………………

91. *Parklive* – Blur

Parklive, just like its near identical predecessors, *All the People: Blur Live at Hyde Park 02/07/09 & 03/07/09*, finds Blur playing live, once again, in Hyde Park. The albums were released just three years apart, and in that time nothing has really changed. *Parklive* didn't really need to be released, it was put out, again, like its predecessors, to mark the occasion, this time, the cultural significance of Blur's role in the London Olympic games.

The album sneaked into the top 100 at number 91, but again, that didn't really matter. The presence of Ed Sheeran, amongst others, in the top 10 with his debut album +, showed that thoughtful indie-rock music, influenced by Blur, was still around, and it would only be a year away that Sheeran would become the biggest act in the world. Elbow too, sort of contemporaries to Blur, were also in the top 10, with their mega hit album, the Mercury Prize winning, *The Seldom Seen Kid*, meaning that there was still a place for Blur, or an act like them, in the UK music scene.

Fast forward another three years, and bolstered by the huge success of their come-back, the band chose to do something that no-one thought they would back in 2003, and that was to make another album.

Movin' On

Album 8:

The Magic Whip
Released: 27th April 2015; UK Chart Positions: 1;
Label: Parlophone/Warner Brothers
Track Listing: Lonesome Street; New World Towers; Go Out; Ice Cream Man; thought I Was a Spaceman; I Broadcast; My Terracotta Heart; There Are Too Many of Us; Ghost Ship; Pyongyang; On Ong; Mirrorball
Producer: Stephen Street, Graham Coxon, Damon Albarn

UK Official Albums Chart – Top 10 – 3rd May 2015:

1. ***The Magic Whip* – Blur**
2. *1989* – Taylor Swift
3. *Chaos and the Calm* – James Bay
4. *Stages* – Josh Groban
5. *Title* – Meghan Trainor
6. *The Ultimate Collection* – Paul Simon
7. *X* – Ed Sheeran
8. *In the Lonely Hour* – Sam Smith
9. *Wanted on Voyage* – George Ezra
10. *Smoke & Mirrors* – Imagine Dragons

By 2015, Blur was no longer Damon Albarn's day job. That was now Gorillaz. The collective of musicians grouped together under the loose banner of a fictitious band managed to scratch Albarn's many musical itches, and gave him the opportunity of writing and playing with a whole host of artists, whilst keeping his own celebrity somewhere in the background. Damon has really let himself wallow in his work with Gorillaz over the years, with an incredible output that includes eight albums between 2001 and 2020. To put it in context, worldwide, Gorillaz have sold 18 million albums to Blur's 15 million. And that doesn't include the two albums due out in late 2020.

So, when Damon suggested a new Blur album back in 2015, he was at least free of the constraints of pressure associated with writing an album that needed to sell so that the band could eat. Blur's priorities had shifted, and this put the band, and the album, in a position of power. They could go anywhere, write and record anything, and be whatever they wanted to be. They chose to stay in London and record at 13.

Well, that's not entirely true. Recording began in Hong Kong purely by accident, after the band found themselves stranded for five days in May 2013 when the Tokyo Rocks music festival was cancelled at short notice. With nothing else to do, they laid down a bunch of tracks in Avon Studios, thinking that nothing would come of it. Damon then went about touring his solo album (2014's *Everyday Robots*) and Graham quietly slipped into 13 with Blur's old producer Stephen Street and worked on the tracks. The pair finally presented them to Damon and the rest of the band in 2014, and on his way back from Australia, Damon stopped off once more in Hong Kong to write the lyrics, and the album was finished by January 2015, the production credits shared between Street, Graham and Damon. The Chinese influence can be seen on the album's cover, the title and the band's name are written in Chinese text.

The Magic Whip

Where *Think Tank* failed to play on its Moroccan influences, having been predominately written in drizzly London, its successor, separated by thousands of miles and 12 years, does its best to connect with its Chinese influence. Tracks like Pyongyang and Ong Ong make direct reference, whilst My Terracotta Heart draws on the legend of the Terracotta warriors, buried to guard the tomb of the first emperor of a unified China, Qin Shi Huang, who gave his name, Qin, to his country.

Blur were not known in Hong Kong, or in mainland China, certainly not like they were in Japan, and Avon Studios was a relatively tiny spot for such a well-established band to record in. Once again they are reconnecting with their roots, just as they did with *Blur*. Not by listening to lo-fi American punk music, but in taking the weight of their history, their success, and their individual public characters out of the equation. Of all the ways they could have gone with a new album, it was as if they were asking themselves the question: what would we do if we could restart the band again from scratch, but knowing what we know now?

Stylistically the album picks up from where Under the Westway left off, with Damon's plodding keyboard lines augmented by Graham's twiddly guitar parts, Alex and Dave holding up the rhythm section with their typical pose. Album opener Lonesome Street is classic Blur of *Parklife* era, clanging minor7 chords marching on as Damon sings about undergrounds and "The five fourteen to East Grinstead" in his best Ray Davies impression (Lonesome Street is presumably just around the corner from Dead End Street). Just like Tender, Graham adds his own second half to the verse, singing alongside Damon and harmonising with himself, positioning himself firmly back in the passenger seat that he vacated briefly for *Think Tank*.

The Magic Whip wouldn't win the band any new fans, but then it wasn't designed to. New World Towers doesn't even have a chorus, but it doesn't matter, because Blur had proved themselves again and again, and with their return to the live forum in 2009, it was clear that their audience was still there, and would accept whatever they pushed their way.

Lyrically the album returns Albarn to his heyday of *Modern Life is Rubbish* and *Parklife*, as he draws together clutches of references to London and any urban areas, sly references to China and the far east consistently popping up through references to neon, both in the lyrics and in the album's artwork. The far east had long been synonymous with neon lights, and Damon uses the image to widen the story of what might otherwise be thought of as a purely London one, considering the band's connections to the UK capital. The first track released to promote the album was Go Out, a dirgy fuzz box led number that wouldn't have been out of place on *Blur*, continues the neon light imagery, this time drawing in the darker, more seedier aspect that the idea of neon lights brings, the infamous Hong Kong underworld:

Too many Western men, Top button left undone
Imperious their signs
The pedlars of luxury
A greedy go-getter in the sky bar

Five tracks from the total of 12 were released as singles. Although in the age of streaming playing the lead role in the charts, it was no longer clear what 'released' really meant. Only Go Out and Lonesome Street found their way into the lower reaches of the top 200, peaking at 182 and 151 respectively. But again, the fact the album went straight into number 1 meant that this had no bearing on the strength of the album at all. This meant that it was Blur's clearest concept album since *Parklife*, much more so than the collection of songs that *The Great Escape* was, for example. The power of streaming meant that bands have needed to rethink what tracks were released in what order, but for all the accessibility, the years that Blur had put into their work by this juncture meant that people trusted the curation that the band would put into an album, listening to it as a whole, not picking out individual tracks, which again, was what helped let *The Great Escape* down.

That is not to say that the album doesn't have high and low points though, and the deep electronica of Thought I was a Spaceman slips into the realms of self-indulgence. After the clanging guitars of the first four tracks, the album takes its delve into modern electronica seriously, positioning itself like nearly all of Blur's previous albums – heavily weighted toward the first half of the record. Although, the bleeps on My Terracotta Heart sit very comfortably alongside Damon's finger picked acoustic guitar, and Graham's chromatic scale licks, plus There Are Too Many of Us, a somewhat obvious nod to over-population (another China reference?), is a slow builder that proves itself to be one of the best on the album, a more militant update on The Universal.

There are few surprises on *The Magic Whip*, it is perhaps the exact record that you might expect Damon et al to record at this point in their careers. To fans of the band it plays well and fits seamlessly into their canon without pushing them forward with any great leaps or bounds. Damon had learned the difficulty with positioning his band at the vanguard of exploring new ground, both lyrically and sonically, when *The Great Escape* divided its audience so clearly, and the band are careful to fit *The Magic Whip* into the contemporary music world without either appearing old and out of touch, or pushing the experimental angle too much, like perhaps Radiohead were, and are still, doing. It's a good album, but partly because of how understated it is, it is tough to see how it will be the last Blur album, surely there will be another one.

To the End

Since *The Magic Whip* and the subsequent world tour that wrapped up in the United Arab Emirates (there can't be too many Western bands to play the UAE), Blur have been on another hiatus of sorts. In 2019 they came out of hiding to play a one off gig as part of the line-up for Africa Express, a collective of African and Western artists, started by Damon Albarn in 2006, in the London Borough of Waltham Forest, where Damon lived before moving to Colchester. Also on the bill, amongst the likes of Django Django and Joan as Police Woman, was one of Damon's other projects, The Good, The Bad & The Queen. The event and the performances was yet another example of Damon's philanthropy, of giving something back to the community he was from, but also his proliferation outside of Blur, as well as his permanent fixture in the UK arts scene.

Where Gorillaz plan to tour the UK and Europe throughout December 2020 and June/July 2021 (COVID-19 pending), and Damon has his own solo tour planed for March 2021, Blur have no upcoming shows booked, and no plans to record together again. But that doesn't mean that they won't.

Damon of course keeps himself in the public eye and rarely a day seems to go by when he hasn't popped up with yet another musical project on the go. Graham has returned to Camden, splitting his time between London and LA, to continue working on his TV soundtrack work. Alongside the first two series of *The End of the F***ing World*, he has also added *I Am Not Okay with This* in 2020 to his roster. The show is another superpower based coming-of-age teen drama set also in LA.

Dave Rowntree, aside from hosting various XFM shows over the years, gaining his advanced pilots licence in 2016, and finally won a seat as a county councillor for Norwich in 2017; so is dedicating his life to politics, just on a much more local scale than he had once planned. After all the extravagance of his twenties and thirties Alex James now lives a quiet life making cheese and attending and running food festivals in Kingham in Oxfordshire with his wife of seventeen years and their five children.

Although each of their fates seems to perfectly fit the characters that the fans came to know over the years, the band seem to lead such disparate lives to one another, and it is almost impossible to understand how they came together in the first place. In his book, Alex James hits the nail on the head when he says, "I often acted as a mediator between Damon and Graham. My blasé temperament was a pivot for them both and perhaps it suggested an underlying harmony in an arrangement that might otherwise have collapsed."[xli]

Damon also understood this to both his detriment, and then later on, to his credit. Firstly, when Graham was asked to leave the band in 2003, Damon – perhaps somewhat misguidedly – considered that Blur was bigger than any of its individual members and needed to move forward to survive, even if it meant without one of its members. One of the four members that have only ever been part of Blur. This is perhaps why *Think Tank* is tinged with such a melancholic undertone. The band were missing their friend, and it shows in the music.

Then later, when the band reformed in 2009, Damon also showed that he understood Blur's key strength to be the interpersonal relationships between the four members. Just as Alex says, each of their characters helps to augment the relationships between the whole, that otherwise might not have worked. Damon didn't need to put the band back together in order to pay the bills (as many other acts were forced to do around this time after streaming meant the bottom fell out of the album sales market), Gorillaz had made him a very rich man, and were far more successful than Blur would ever be. What he understood though was that Blur's essence came when these four people played together. It is why the songs are credited to all four members, despite it being Damon that mostly brought into the room the chord sequence and basic structure of what could be called 'the song'. The lyrics are then credited to whoever writes them, generally Damon, but more commonly as the band continued, Graham. Alex James also got a credit for Far Out on *Parklife*, as well as a couple of B-sides.

Coldplay do a similar thing, but where there is no doubt that they are Chris Martin and some other people, Blur, despite Damon being the leader, are the four members of the band, each bringing their own strength to the table to make the group what it is. Julian Opie understood this with his portrait of them for their best-of album, the artist managing to capture the essence of what makes them, them.

The solidarity within the band made them brothers, the band and what it achieved permanently connecting them with each other in the public conscious, but also in their own consciousness. Success in music is often about timing, and Blur came along at a time that both defined them, and also kept them trapped within it. In trying to break free from the shackles of Britpop and the mid-nineties, we saw a band that were forced to find ways to define themselves on another level in order to survive. Setting the cartoons aside for a moment, Gorillaz are a project run by an incredibly talented musician and have proved their worth with their staggering success. But success is not just registered in record sales, Spotify streams or You Tube videos, what Blur understood, and what their audience understands about them today is that they are four members, the unit greater than the sum of its parts, that managed to capture a moment in time when it mattered to be where they were.

The music is only part of it. It's the reason that groups have names, rather than just being called Damon, Graham, Alex and Dave. Despite the band only ever having consisted of those four people, the group needs a name, because it stands for something more than the four members can offer. Bands belong to their audience, the music their way of transmitting the feeling of seeing them play or listening to their records. Blur are one of the greatest British groups of all time because of what they mean to their audience, and what they mean to the time and place that they played in and the impact that has had on British culture, not just in Britain, but around the world.

Perhaps not the first band that comes to people's lips when they think of the greatest British bands, they manage to bridge the near impossible gap of enormous popularity and indie credibility like no other band before, or perhaps ever will again. Quite the feat for four lads who left their hometowns to experience the world, and ended up on *Top of the Pops*.

THE END

ABOUT THE AUTHOR

Tom Boniface-Webb is a writer and sometime filmmaker from Reading in the South-East of the United Kingdom. He currently lives in Wellington, New Zealand.

In 2017 his first non-fiction book 'I Was Britpopped: The A-Z of Britpop' was published through Valley Press, written with the co-author Jenny Natasha.
'Modern Music Masters – Oasis' was published in October 2020.

For more information about the Modern Music Masters series:
modernmusicmastersuk@gmail.com
www.modernmusicmasters.co.uk

APPENDIX:

Blur are one of those bands (Oasis are not) who released a lot of material as limited edition, import only, or made available only to their fan club. The numbers that these releases were put out in means that they were often ineligible for the charts, and as such have not been included as part of the official releases above. Below is a list of as many of these limited edition releases as I could find.

I have chosen not to included Boxed Sets, because these are just a collection of all of the band's singles, or albums, all in one place, and as such, not a particularly interesting limited edition or important only release.

However, for completion, there are two major boxed sets: *The 10 Year Ltd. Edition Anniversary Box Set* – which included all of the band's singles between 1991 and 1999; and *Blur 21* – which included all of their releases between 1991 and 2012.

In no particular order. Thanks to www.discogs.com the best resource for all official and unofficial music releases.

Live Album:

Live at the Budokan – 8th & 9th November 1995
Released: 22nd May 1996 – Japan only; UK Chart Positions: n/a; Label: Food Records
Track Listing: CD1: The Great Escape; Jubilee; Popscene; End of a Century; Tracy Jacks; Mr. Robinson's Quango; To the End; Fade Away; It Could Be You; Stereotypes; She's So High; Girls & Boys; Advert; Intermission; Bank Holiday; For Tomorrow; Country House; This Is a Low; Supa Shoppa
CD2: Yuko and Hiro; He Thought of Cars; Coping; Globe Alone; Parklife; The Universal

Producer: Blur

B-sides Album:

The Special Collectors Edition
Released: 26th October 1994 – Japan only; UK Chart Positions: n/a; Label: Food Records
Track Listing: Day Upon Day (Live at Moles Club, Bath, 19 December 1990); Inertia; Luminous; Mace; Badgeman Brown; Hanging Over; Peach; When the Cows Come Home; Maggie May; Es Schmecht; Fried; Anniversary Waltz; Threadneedle Street; Got Yer!; Supa Shoppa; Beard; Theme from an Imaginary Film; Bank Holiday
Producer: Stephen Street, Steve Lovell, Blur and John Smith

Promo Single 1:

High Cool (Easy Listening Mix)/Bad Day (Leisurely Mix)
Released: 11th November 1991 – UK only; Label: Food Records; Format: 12"; ltd. to: 1000 copies
Track Listing: High Cool (Easy Listening Mix); Bad Day (Leisurely Mix)
Producer/remixer: Stephen Street

Promo Single 2:

Blur-ti-go (released by their US label without the band's permission)
Released: 1992 – US only; Label: Food/SBK Records; Format: CD/12"

Track Listing: Bang (Now Mix); Bang (Trend Mix); She's So High (Live); Come Together (Live); Fool (Live); Popscene (Live)
Producer/remixer: Timoth Powell

Promo Single 3 (Christmas Freebie):

The Wassailing Song (trad.)
Released: 15th Dec 1992 – given away free in the pub; Label: Food Records; Format: 7"; ltd. to: 500
Track Listing: The Wassaiiling Song
Performed by: Gold Frankincense and Blur

Promo Single 4:

Bet Bet Bet (recorded at the Mark Radcliffe Session)
Released: 1994 – France only/2019 – UK; Label: Food Records/EMI France; Format: 1994 – CD/2019 – 10"
Track Listing: Girls & Boys; Jubilee; Trouble in the Message Centre; Lot 105
Engineer: Chris Lee

Live Album:

In Concert: New Rock (Recorded live at Glastonbury Festival 1994)
Released: 12th September 1994; Label: Westwood One; Format: CD
Track Listing: Jubilee; Tracy Jacks; Magic America; End of the Century; Chemical World; There's No Other Way; Parklife; Girls & Boys; Bank Holiday
Engineer: Doug Field

Promo Single 5:

Entertain Me (The Live It! remix)
Released: 1995 – US only; Label: EMI America; Format: 12"
Track Listing: Entertain Me (The Live It! remix)
Producer: Stephen Street; Remixer: Live It!

Promo Single 6:

This is a Low
Released: 5th January 1995 – Japan only; Label: Food Records; Format: CD
Track Listing: This is a Low
Producer: Stephen Street

Live Album:

Planet – Live! (recorded live at Wembley Arena, 13th December 1995)
Released: 1996 – Australia only; Label: Austereo MFC; Format: CD
Track Listing: The Great Escape; It Could Be You; Tracy Jacks; Jingle Bells; Stereotypes; End of the Century; Charmless Man; Coping; Mr. Robinson's Quango; Mack The Knife; Jubilee; To the End; She`s So High; Sunday Sunday; Advert' Bank Holiday; Supa Shoppa; Country House; Girls & Boys; He Thought Of Cars/Encore; Globe Alone; This Is A Low; My Sharona; Parklife; Beard; For Tomorrow; The Universal; Interview Cut A; Interview Cut B
Producer: Blur

Promo Single 7:

Death of a Party
Released: 1996 – fan club only; Label: Food Records; Format: CD
Track Listing: Death of a Party (1992 demo version)
Producer: Blur

Promo Single 8:

It Could be You
Released: 22nd May 1996 – Japan only; Label: Food/EMI Records; Format: CD
Track Listing: It Could be You (album version); It Could be You (live in Budokon); Charmless Man (live in Budokon); Chemical World (live in Budokon)
Producer: Stephen Street

Promo Single 9:

I Love Her
Released: October 1997 – fan club only; Label: Food/EMI Records; Format: CD
Track Listing: I Love Her (recorded in 1991)
Producer: Blur

Promo Single 10:

Live (recorded live in Muziekcentrum Vredenburg, Utrecht)
Released: 22nd September 1997 – Holland only; Label: EMI Records; Format: CD
Track Listing: Country Sad Ballad Man; M.O.R.; Popscene; Death of a Party; Song 2; On Your Own

Engineers: Arjen Arwert & Thijs Peters

Promo Single 11:

Close
Released: 1998 – fan club only; Label: Food Records/Parlophone; Format: CD
Track Listing: Close (recorded in 1992)
Producers: Stephen Street & John Smith

Promo Single 12:

Bugman Promo 1
Released: 1999; Label: Food Records/Parlophone; Format: CD
Track Listing: Trade Stylee (Alex's Bugman Remix); Metal Hip Slop (Graham's Bugman Remix); X-Offender (Damon/Control Freaks Bugman Remix); Coyote (Dave's Bugman Remix)
Producer: William Orbit

Promo Single 13:

Bugman Promo 2
Released: 1999; Label: Food Records; Format: 12"
Track Listing: Bugman (William Orbit Remix); Bugman (Alex's Remix); Bugman (Graham's Remix)
Producer: William Orbit

Promo Single 14:

Sing (to Me)

Released: 1999 – fan club only; Label: Food Records; Format: CD
Track Listing: Sing (to Me) [recorded in 1989 or 1990]
Producer: Graeme Holdaway

Promo Single 15:

B-Sides Gig E.P (recorded live at the Electric Ballroom, Camden – 6th Sept 1999)
Released: 2001 – fan club only; Label: EMI Records; Format: CD
Track Listing: I'm Fine; Bone Bag; No Monsters in Me; Young + Lovely
Engineer: Matt Butcher

Promo Single 16:

Don't Bomb When You're the Bomb
Released: 13th November 2002; Label: MSP (self-released); Format: 7"/12"; Ltd. to: 1000 copies
Track Listing: Don't Bomb When You're the Bomb
Producer: Blur

Promo Single 17:

Won't Do It/Come Together
Released: April 2002 – fan club only; Label: Parlophone; Format: CD
Track Listing: Won't Do It (demo)/Come Together (demo)
Producer: Blur

Promo Single 18:

Colours
Released: 28th August 2003 – fan club only; Label: EMI Records; Format: CD
Track Listing: Colours
Producer: Ben Hillier

Promo Single 19:

Me, White Noise
Released: 2003 – Holland only; Label: EMI Uden; Format: CD
Track Listing: Me, White Noise
Producer: Ben Hillier

Promo Single 20:

We've Got a File on You
Released: April 2003 – white label; Label: Virgin; Format: 7"; ltd. to: 1000 copies
Track Listing: We've Got a File on You
Producer: Ben Hellier

Promo Single 21:

Some Glad Morning
Released: December 2005 – fan club only; Label: Parlophone; Format: CD
Track Listing: Some Glad Morning
Producer: Ben Hellier

Promo Single 22:

Fool's Day

Released: 17th April 2010 – for Record Store Day only; Label: Parlophone; Format: 7"; ltd. to: 1000 copies (3000 later pressed in the US)
Track Listing: Fool's Day
Producer: Blur

Promo Single 23:

Ong Ong
Released: 2015; Label: Parlophone; Format: CD
Track Listing: Ong Ong; Ong Ong (instrumental)
Producer: Stephen Street, Graham Coxon, Damon Albarn

Promo Single 24:

Y'All Doomed
Released: 2015; Label: Parlophone; Format: 7"
Track Listing: Y'All Doomed
Producer: Stephen Street, Graham Coxon, Damon Albarn

Promo Single 25:

Lonesome Street
Released: 2015; Label: Parlophone; Format: CD
Track Listing: Lonesome Street (radio edit); Lonesome Street (album version); Lonesome Street (instrumental)
Producer: Stephen Street, Graham Coxon, Damon Albarn

Promo Single 26:

Ghost Ship
Released: September 2015; Label: Parlophone; Format: CD
Track Listing: Ghost Ship
Producer: Stephen Street, Graham Coxon, Damon Albarn

---

[i] Alex James quoted in *No Distance Left to Run*
[ii] James, Alex 'Bit of a Blur' pg. 29, Little, Brown (2007)
[iii] NME quote - https://web.archive.org/web/20000817223029/http://www.nme.com/reviews/reviews/19980101001044reviews.html
[iv] James, Alex 'Bit of a Blur' pg. 61, Little, Brown (2007)
[v] Quoted in - http://www.vblurpage.com/articles/stories/sos_99.htm
[vi] https://www.nme.com/photos/the-500-greatest-albums-of-all-time-100-1-1426116
[vii] NME quote - https://web.archive.org/web/20000817223029/http://www.nme.com/reviews/reviews/19980101001044reviews.html
[viii] Quoted in 'No Distance Left to Run' (2009)
[ix] James, Alex 'Bit of a Blur' pg. 110, Little, Brown (2007)
[x] Quote - http://www.sanderswood.com/press/view/press_images/19950120.sexads.men.jpg.html
[xi] Source - https://www.officialcharts.com/chart-news/official-charts-flashback-1994-blur-parklife__4770/
[xii] Amis, Martin 'London Fields' pg. 4, Vintage (2003)
[xiii] Source - https://www.officialcharts.com/chart-news/official-charts-flashback-1994-blur-parklife__4770/
[xiv] James, Alex 'Bit of a Blur' pg. 123, Little, Brown (2007)
[xv] Quoted from an interview with Mat Whitecross, director of the Oasis documentary *Supersonic*
[xvi] All Blur sales figures taken from - http://www.vblurpage.com/info/chartography/sales_albums.htm
[xvii] The Telegraph, Paul, Clements (10 December 2008). "Blur: the Britpop boys are back, but do we want them?".
[xviii] Reference - https://www.bbc.co.uk/music/reviews/8qwx/
[xix] Power, Martin 'The Life of Blur', pg. 167, Omnibus Press (2013)
[xx] Reference - https://www.bbc.co.uk/music/reviews/8qwx/
[xxi] Stuart Maconie, "The Death of a Party", Select magazine, (August 1999).
[xxii] Quoted in - https://www.digitalspy.com/music/a46469/damon-albarn-criticises-blur-albums/

[xxiii] Quoted from *No Distance Left to Run*
[xxiv] Quoted from *No Distance Left to Run*
[xxv] *The Last Party* by John Harris, pg. 286
[xxvi] Dave Rowntree quoted in *No Distance Left to Run*
[xxvii] Quoted in - https://www.allmusic.com/album/blur-mw0000082694
[xxviii] *The Last Party*, by John Harris, pg. 323
[xxix] Power, Martin 'The Life of Blur' pg. 217, Omnibus Press (2013)
[xxx] Ginger Baker quoted in Mojo 314, January 2020
[xxxi] Power, Martin 'The Life of Blur' pg. 219, Omnibus Press (2013)
[xxxii] Quoted in - https://www.rockshop.co.nz/shop/digitech-dod-gonkulator-ring-modulator-fx-pedal.html
[xxxiii] Quote in Grays Guitar interview with Graham Coxon and Stephen Street - https://www.youtube.com/watch?v=8n8k0fB82nU
[xxxiv] Power, Martin '*The Life of Blur*', pg. 209, Omnibus (2013)
[xxxv] Quoted in - http://www.vblurpage.com/articles/gigs/meltdown.htm
[xxxvi] Quoted in http://www.rockonthenet.com/artists-g/gorillaz.htm
[xxxvii] Quoted in https://www.webcitation.org/5le8WXHB0?url=http://audio.theguardian.tv/audio/kip/music/series/paul-morley-showing-off/1259329339795/8827/AlbarnMorleyFINAL.mp3
[xxxviii] James, Alex 'A Bit of a Blur', pg. 31, Little, Brown (2007)
[xxxix] James, Alex 'A Bit of a Blur', pg. 121, Little, Brown (2007)
[xl] James, Alex 'A Bit of a Blur', pg. 193, Little, Brown (2007)
[xli] James, Alex 'A Bit of a Blur' pg. 182, Little, Brown (2007)

Made in the USA
Middletown, DE
14 July 2021